Private Gardens

Rockeries to the south of the pond, Yipu Garden
Preceding page

This is the central part of the garden to the south of the lake. The hill, the abundance of trees and flowers and their inverted reflection in the water are a handsome sight. The artificial hill is of earth, and Taihu stones are piled up on the side bordering on the lake forming lofty and steep crags. On the southern side of the hill a small pavilion has been placed, accessible by a path built through the rocks. At the foot of the hill, there is a stone bridge on each side built across the spurs of the lake. These give the impression that the source of the water is far away in the mountains, and the rockery rising steeply out of the water forms a contrast to the gently flowing water in the lake.

The Excellence of Ancient Chinese Architecture

PRIVATE GARDENS

Gardens for the Enjoyment of Artificial
Landscapes of Men of Letters

Cheng Liyao

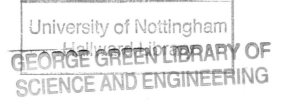
China Architecture & Building Press

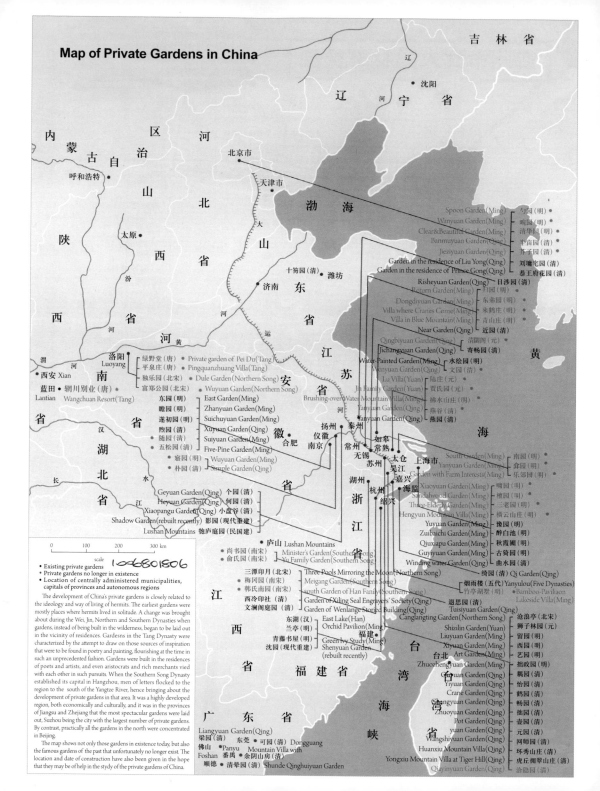

Map of Private Gardens in China

吉林省

辽宁省
·沈阳

河
辽

内蒙古自治区

河北省

渤海

黄海

呼和浩特·

山西省

北京市

天津市

太原·

大山

山东省

河

济南

十笏园(清) 潍坊

黄河

江苏省

运河

陕西省

渭河

西安 Xian

河南省

洛阳 Luoyang

绿野堂(唐) Private garden of Pei Du(Tang)
平泉庄(唐) Pingquanzhuang Villa(Tang)
独乐园(北宋) Dule Garden(Northern Song)
富郑公园(北宋)
Wuyuan Garden(Northern Song)

蓝田 Lantian
辋川别业(唐)
Wangchuan Resort(Tang)

安徽省

合肥

扬州

仪徴
南京

泰州

如皋
常州 常熟
无锡 苏州 太仓 上海市
吴江
嘉兴
海盐

东园(明) East Garden(Ming)
瞻园(明) Zhanyuan Garden(Ming)
遂初园(明) Suichuyuan Garden(Ming)
煦园(清) Xuyuan Garden(Qing)
随园(清) Suiyuan Garden(Ming)
五松园(清) Five-Pine Garden(Qing)
寤园(明) Wuyuan Garden(Ming)
朴园(清) Simple Garden(Qing)

湖北省

长江

江

汉水

Spoon Garden(Ming) 勺园(明)
Wanyuan Garden(Ming) 晚园(明)
Clear&Beautiful Garden(Ming) 清华园(明)
Banmuyuan Garden(Ming) 半亩园(明)
Jieziyuan Garden(Qing) 芥子园(清)
Garden in the residence of Liu Yong(Qing) 刘墉宅园(清)
Garden in the residence of Prince Gong(Qing) 恭王府花园(清)
Risheyuan Garden(Qing) 日涉园(清)
Return Garden(Ming) 归园(明)
Dongdiyuan Garden(Ming) 东弟园(明)
Villa where Cranes Come(Ming) 米鹤庄(明)
Villa in Blue Mountain(Ming) 青山庄(明)
Near Garden(Qing) 近园(清)
Qingbiyuan Garden(Qing) 清閟阁(清)
Jichangyuan Garden(Qing) 寄畅园(清)
Water-Painted Garden(Ming) 水绘园(明)
Wenyuan Garden(Qing) 文园(清)
Lu Villa(Yuan) 陆庄(元)
Jin Family Garden(Yuan) 贾氏园(元)
Brushing-over Water Mountain Villa(Ming) 拂水山庄(明)
Yanyuan Garden(Ming) 燕谷(清)
Yanyuan Garden(Qing) 燕园(清)

South Garden(Ming) 南园(明)
Yanyuan Garden(Ming) 弇园(明)
Garden with Farm Interests(Ming) 乐郊园(明)
Xiaoyuan Garden(Ming) 啸园(明)
Sandalwood Garden(Ming) 檀园(明)
Three-Elderly Garden(Ming) 三老园(明)
Hengyun Mountain Villa(Ming) 横云山庄(明)
Drunkard Garden(Ming) 醉园(明)
Zuibaichi Garden(Ming) 醉白池(明)
Qiuxiapu Garden(Ming) 秋霞圃(明)
Guyiyuan Garden(Ming) 古猗园(明)
Winding water Garden(Qing) 曲水园(清)
Qi Garden(Qing) 绮园(清)

庐山

浙江省

湖州 杭州
绍兴

Geyuan Garden(Qing) 个园(清)
Heyuan Garden(Qing) 何园(清)
Xiaopangu Garden(Qing) 小盘谷(清)
Shadow Garden(rebuilt recently) 影园(现代重建)
Lushan Mountains 匡庐庭园(民国建)

庐山 Lushan Mountains

Minister's Garden(Southern Song) 尚书园(南宋)
Yu Family Garden(Southern Song) 俞氏园(南宋)

Three Pools Mirroring the Moon(Northern Song) 三潭印月(北宋)
Meigang Garden(Southern Song) 梅岗园(南宋)
south Garden of Han Family(Southern Song) 韩氏南园(南宋)
Garden of Xiling Seal Engravers' Society(Qing) 西泠印社(清)
Garden of Wenlange Storing Building(Qing) 文澜阁庭园(清)

Yanyulou(Five Dynasties) 烟雨楼(五代)
Bamboo-Pavilion Lakeside Villa(Ming) 竹亭湖墅(明)
Tuisiyuan Garden(Qing) 退思园(清)

江西省

East Lake(Han) 东湖(汉)
Orchid Pavilion(Ming) 兰亭(明)
Green Ivy Study(Ming) 青藤书屋(明)
Shenyuan Garden (rebuilt recently) 沈园(现代重建)

福建省

台湾省

台北

Canglangting Garden(Northern Song) 沧浪亭(北宋)
Shizilin Garden(Yuan) 狮子林园(元)
Liuyuan Garden(Ming) 留园(明)
Xiyuan Garden(Ming) 西园(明)
Art Garden(Ming) 艺园(明)
Zhuozhengyuan Garden(Ming) 拙政园(明)
Ouyuan Garden(Qing) 耦园(清)
Yiyuan Garden(Qing) 怡园(清)
Crane Garden(Qing) 鹤园(清)
Changyuan Garden(Qing) 畅园(清)
Zhuoyuan Garden(Qing) 拙园(清)
Pot Garden(Qing) 壶园(清)
Wangshiyuan Garden(Qing) 网师园(清)
Huanxiu Mountain Villa(Qing) 环秀山庄(清)
Yongxiu Mountain Villa at Tiger Hill(Qing) 虎丘拥翠山庄(清)
Qiayinyuan Garden(Qing) 洽隐园(清)

广东省

台湾海峡

Liangyuan Garden(Qing) 梁园(清)
佛山 Foshan
东莞 Dongguang
可园(清) Keyuan(Qing)
番禺 Panyu
Mountain Villa with
余阴山房(清)
顺德 Shunde
清晖园(清) Shunde Qinghuiyuan Garden

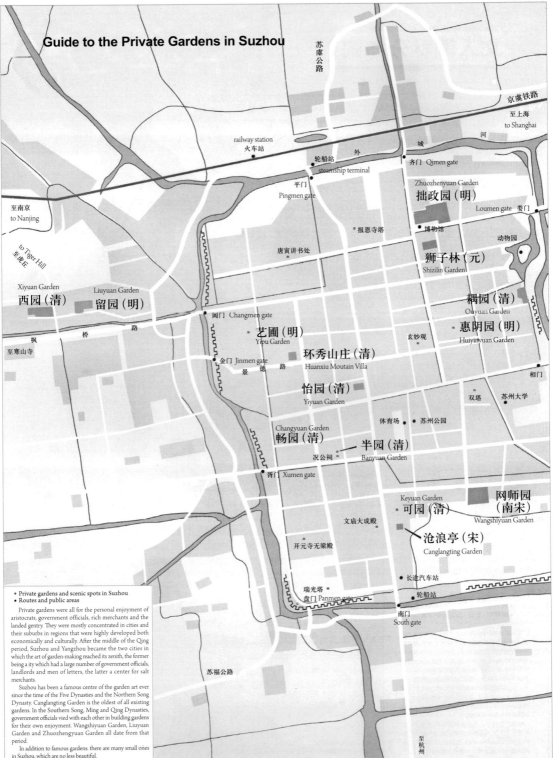

Guide to the Private Gardens in Suzhou

苏廌公路

京廌铁路

至上海
to Shanghai

城 河

railway station
火车站

轮船站
steamship terminal

外

齐门 Qimen gate

平门
Pingmen gate

Zhuozhenyuan Garden

拙政园（明）

至南京
to Nanjing

Loumen gate 娄门

报恩寺塔

博物馆

动物园

to Tiger Hill
至虎丘

唐寅讲书处

狮子林（元）
Shizilin Garden

Xiyuan Garden
西园（清）

Liuyuan Garden
留园（明）

圆门 Changmen gate

艺圃（明）
Yibu Garden

耦园（清）
Ouyuan Garden

玄妙观

惠阴园（明）
Huiyinyuan Garden

至寒山寺

枫 桥 路

金门 Jinmen gate

景 德 路

环秀山庄（清）
Huanxiu Moutain Villa

相门

双塔

苏州大学

怡园（清）
Yiyuan Garden

体育场

苏州公园

Changyuan Garden
畅园（清）

半园（清）
Banyuan Garden

况公祠

齐门 Xumen gate

Keyuan Garden

网师园
（南宋）
Wangshiyuan Garden

可园（清）

文庙大成殿

沧浪亭（宋）
Canglangting Garden

开元寺无梁殿

长途汽车站

瑞光塔

轮船站

盘门 Panmen gate

南门
South gate

苏福公路

至杭州

• Private gardens and scenic spots in Suzhou
• Routes and public areas

Private gardens were all for the personal enjoyment of
aristocrats, government officials, rich merchants and the
landed gentry. They were mostly concentrated in cities and
their suburbs in regions that were highly developed both
economically and culturally. After the middle of the Qing
period, Suzhou and Yangzhou became the two cities in
which the art of garden-making reached its zenith, the former
being a ity which had a large number of government officials,
landlords and men of letters, the latter a center for salt
merchants.

Suzhou has been a famous centre of the garden art ever
since the time of the Five Dynasties and the Northern Song
Dynasty. Canglangting Garden is the oldest of all existing
gardens. In the Southern Song, Ming and Qing Dynasties,
government officials vied with each other in building gardens
for their own enjoyment. Wangshiyuan Garden, Liuyuan
Garden and Zhuozhengyuan Garden all date from that
period.

In addition to famous gardens, there are many small ones
in Suzhou, which are no less beautiful.

Contents

General Introduction

Notes on the Photographs

Jiangsu Province

5

Shanghai

Zhejiang Province

Guangdong Province

Appendices

Editor's Note

- The series consists of ten volumes, each of which deals with respectively palace architecture, imperial mausoleums, imperial gardens, private gardens, vernacular dwellings, Buddhist buildings, Taoist buildings, Islamic buildings, ritual and ceremonious buildings and defense structures..

- Each volume is basically composed of four sections, i.e. general introduction, colour photographs, glossary and chronology of major events.

- The general introduction describes the background, development process, architectural characteristics of different types of buildings and is complimented with photographs and drawings.

- The colour photographs are arranged in the order of building distribution area or the time when the building was completed. The series contains about 1,700 exquisite colour photographs, which are attached with captions explaining the location, construction time, and artistic and technical features.

- Each volume is accompanied with layout plan, drawing of recovered buildings, distribution map and travel guide to mark the location of famous buildings and cultural attractions in the vicinity.

- The glossary is arrayed according to the sequence of strokes of Chinese characters, which is a reference for general readers.

- Chronology of major events is affiliated with each volume of the series. Chinese traditional chronology is adopted in the annals of the series, and is also indicated in the Christian era for easy reference.

Preface 1

China enjoys a long and profound history of ancient architecture. Her verifiable artifacts could be dated back to 7,000 years ago from Hemudu ruins in Yuyao to Banpo ruins in Xi'an. Of course, architecture underwent a long process from primitiveness to sophistication before the Warring States, while in the Qin and Han dynasties, it gained an apparent progress along with the development of production and unification of the country. Moreover, in over a thousand years of the prosperous Tang Dynasty to the Ming and Qing dynasties, it reached several unprecedented peaks which were embodied by diversified building forms and refined planning and exquisite construction.

The love of architecture is the love of history and culture. China Architecture & Building Press (CABP), from the very beginning of its founding, has defined the sorting out and publication of traditional Chinese architecture and the enhancement of Chinese culture as one of important themes in its mission. In 1950s and 1960s, many monographs on the subject by experts such as Liang Sicheng, Liu Dunzhen, Tong Jun, Liu Zhiping and others were published. In early 1980s when China was just opened to the outside world, CABP set aside a special fund for publication of academic books on ancient Chinese architecture despite of the limited financial capability then. As a result, large academic albums of Ancient *Chinese Architecture, Ancient Architecture in Chengde, the Art of Chinese Gardens, the Buildings of Confucius Temple in Qufu, Ancient Buildings of Putuoshan, Summer Palace as well as* five volumes of *History of Ancient Chinese Architecture* were put forth continuously. Those books have proved to be of high academic and practical values in consolidation, conservation and protection of the national treasure.

The Excellence of Ancient Chinese Architecture in English is a series of ten volumes on various aspects of the ancient Chinese architecture, which offer a comprehensive coverage of the art, highlighted by the supreme quality of the photos as well as plenty of drawings of plans, sections and perspectives. The easy description would lead to a comprehension of the cultural essence of Chinese architecture, and appreciation of the aesthetics and philosophy embodied by the art. The authors are famous Chinese experts who have long been engaged in the study of the related subjects, whose dedication makes the series authoritative and informative for interested laymen and specialists alike. Now the Excellence of Ancient Chinese Architecture is published. It is a happy event. I believe that it will serve as a door for all those who are interested in the study of ancient Chinese architecture.

Zhou Yi | Former President
China Architecture & Building Press

Former Chairman, Committee on Publication
of Science Books
Vice Chairman, Chinese Association of Publishers

Preface 2

As history advances in the new era of the 21st century, China is once again becoming the focus of worldwide attention. The rich variety of her landscape, the wisdom of her people, the current unprecedented economic growth, and the wealth of her cultural heritage are all becoming the subject of worldwide interest.

In China's extensive and profound cultural treasury, ancient architecture is one of the important components, which, in a sense, is of a symbolic nature. The beauty and elegance of ancient Chinese architecture has a uniqueness of its own in the world architectural system. The strict formality of the city layouts, the lively arrangement of village settlements, the grouping of buildings around courtyards, the comprehensive building code for wood structures, the great variety of colour and architectural form, the perfect harmony of the decorative and structural functions of building elements, the integration of furniture, interior decoration, painting, sculpture and calligraphy into a comprehensive art of architecture, all go to manifest the distinctive characteristics of the traditional Chinese culture. A perusal of the country's magnificent palaces and temples, her tranquil and intricate gardens, the wide variety of her vernacular dwellings, and the exquisiteness of her pavilions and roofed walkways, will lead to a better understanding of China and her people. When one comes to study China's ancient architecture, he will have a deeper comprehension of the oriental philosophy of the "oneness of nature and man" inherent in the architectural forms, as well as of the Chinese people's respect for Confucianism, the expression of their philosophical meditation on time and space through material forms, and their all-embracing aesthetic tastes.

Now the Excellence of Ancient Chinese Architecture is published. I believe the vivid and colourful photos will render our readers an enjoyment of aesthetics, and the easy descriptions will facilitate our readers in understanding the cultural essence of ancient Chinese architecture. Under the trend of globalization, it will surely promote the academic exchange internationally and deepen the cultural cooperation among different peoples of the world.

Ye Rutang | Former Vice Minister
Ministry of Construction

The Excellence of Ancient Chinese Architecture

Private Gardens

General Introduction

Development of Private Gardens

—— The garden as a means of seclusion, freeing man from his
worldly cares in order that he may gain a clearer vision of the truth

China's private gardens emerged slightly later than that of the imperial gardens, and it was during the Han Dynasty (206 B.C.- 220 A.D.) that the nobility and high-ranking officials began to have gardens laid out for their own pleasure. These were modelled on the imperial gardens, but were smaller in scale. By the time of the Southern and Northern dynasties (420 A.D. - 589 A.D.), while those in power or in the emperor's favour were vying each other in the building of grand residences and gardens, men of letters began to seek refuge in the pastoral life in order to avoid the social and political turmoil. In the meantime, the rise of "mountain-and-water" or landscape painting and "mountain-and-water" literature as well as the prevalence of Taoism was beginning to have an important impact on the development of private gardens, and as a result they began to shake off the influence of the grandiose and sophisticated style of imperial palaces and gardens.

I. The Hermit and Private Gardens

Private gardens emerged from China's "hermit culture", which lasted as long as her feudal age. If we count the brothers Boyi and Shuqi of the Shang Dynasty in the 11th century B.C. as the forerunners of this special social stratum, the phenomenon of "the hermit" continued till the Ming (1368-1644) and Qing (1644-1911) dynasties, therefore lasting for almost 3,000 years. In spite of the fact that there were only a very limited number of hermits throughout feudal history, they nevertheless played an important role in the development of Chinese culture. Gifted people, famous poets and painters counted among their ranks, and they were always held in high esteem.

1. The Emergence of Hermits and the Development of this Particular Phenomenon

The emergence of hermits was due to a great variety of reasons, but

Scenery on the northern side of the lake in Jichangyuan Garden

First built in the Zhengde reign (1506 – 1510) of the Ming Dynasty and ruined in 1860 during the Qing Dynasty, this garden has now been restored to its original state, although the buildings in the southern part no longer exist. With the lake and the hills on its west side as the focal point, Jichangyuan Garden presents a balanced layout of water and hills. The bridge, hugging the water, connects the eastern and northern banks of the lake. The aim of introducing poetic and painterly concepts in private gardens is achieved to full effect.

generally speaking, men of letters took to withdrawing from society in times of social and political upheaval in order to retain their moral integrity. Boyi and Shuqi were two brothers from a noble family living during the Shang Dynasty (2100 B.C.- 1600 B.C.), and when Shang was overthrown by the Zhou Dynasty (Western Zhou Dynasty: 1100B.C. - 771B.C.), they escaped into the Shouyang Mountains, refused to eat "Zhou Dynasty grain", and finally starved to death. They were, as a result, eulogized as men of high moral principle.

A large number of hermits emerged at the time of Wang Mang (9 A.D.- 23 A.D.), the usurper of the Han Dynasty throne, refusing to cooperate with the new potentate. Another type of hermit was the man of letters, interested in a leisurely and solitary life, and keeping himself aloof from material pursuits. Although he was profoundly learned, he refused steadfastly an official career. Zhuang Zhou of the Spring and Autumn (770-476 B.C.) and Warring States (475-221B.C.) period was the earliest representative of this type of hermit. He regarded officialdom and material riches as dust. "The seven worthies in the bamboo forest" of the Jin Dynasty (265- 420 A.D.), including Ji Kang, Shan Tao, Ruan Ji and several others, were the most famous of this special social stratum. They were all highly learned, talented men, who believed in Taoism and refused to serve the government. Their rebellious spirit in the face of the prevailing ethics was highly praised by other men of letters.

The ruling class was corrupt, avaricious and bloodthirsty, and intellectuals often fell victim to persecution. This was the reason why many men of letters escaped into the mountains, and lived in the holes of trees or in caves. Life was hard and full of danger, yet nature on the other hand gave them great spiritual satisfaction, and provided a source of inspiration for their artistic and literary experiments.

Tao Qian, the most famous scholar and hermit at the end of the Jin Dynasty, was the model for the literati through the ages. He was at one time a county magistrate. Refusing to bow to the powerful and the influential and beg for his salary of five dou of grain (1 dou = 1 decilitre), he served only for eighty days, took off his official hat and left his post. In his famous Return to the Native Field he wrote, "By nature I love the mountains; by mistake I fell victim to worldly dust. Encaged in such custody for thirty years, I at last returned to the embrace of nature." This was the voice close to the hermit's heart.

During the Jin Dynasty, not only did men like Tao Qian seek refuge in nature, but members of influential families fled from the social chaos as well. These men of nobility were in possession of both land and wealth, and their withdrawal from the world brought a change in the form of hermitage. The famous mountain-and-water poet Xie Lingyun, for example, was a descendant of an eminent aristocratic family. In his Rhapsody on Celestial Land, he described four forms of hermitage, namely: "dwelling by rocks", "residence in mountains", "garden in hilly land", and "habitation near cities". Interestingly, none of these four types suggested hermitage in the wilds; they were all havens located in an environment of natural beauty. Hermits could enjoy the pleasures bestowed by nature while having at their disposal the comforts of an otherwise urban life. Their lives had nothing in common with Tao Qian's life of privation and destitution.

The search for beautiful mountains was often considered paramount, and the discovery of many of China's famous mountains, such as the Emei, Lushan, Wuyi, Huashan, and Hengshan Mountains can be ascribed to this determination to find natural beauty, which could console their hearts and provide a source of inspiration leading to many of them becoming famous poets and painters.

2. The Impact of Landscape Painting on Private Gardens

The "mountain-and-water" poetry and pastoral poetry that began to be written during the Wei, Jin, and Southern and Northern dynasties, and the most

important school of Chinese painting, the "mountain-and-water" or landscape painting, which began a little later, were the most important achievements of "hermit culture". The motif of hermit poetry and painting was without exception praise of the beauty of nature and the bliss of the hermit's life. Light breezes over rivers and lakes and the moonshine over mountains were the eternal themes of "mountain-and-water" poetry. This awakening to the beauty of nature was a specific feature of Chinese culture, and the emergence of the private gardens one of its most significant results. The integration of poetry and painting led not only to China's particular mode of garden building, but brought into being the most exquisite artificial environment ever created by mankind.

The "mountain-and-water" school of painting also began during the Wei and Jin dynasties. Looking at the Five Peaks through Dispersing Clouds by Gu Kaizhi of Jin was the first of this type of painting. It gradually matured through the Southern and Northern dynasties and the Sui (581-618) and Tang (618-907) dynasties, and became the mainstream of Chinese painting. The most famous painters were practically all hermits. As with the poets, painters painted not to show or to sell, but purely for their own recreation. The famous artist Zong Bing, who was too old to travel to famous mountains at the time, he had his own paintings, which were actually records of his travels, hung on the four walls of his room so that he could enjoy the beautiful scenery while sitting or lying in

Zhao Mengfu copying Buddhist Scripture and drinking tea with a monk; section of a painting by Qiu Ying

Qiu Ying was one of the four great painters of the Ming Dynasty. In the picture, Zhao Mengfu, a famous Yuan painter and calligrapher, is copying a Buddhist scripture while drinking tea with a monk. Writing, painting, composing poems, drinking tea, chanting Buddhist scripture and roaming through mountains and along rivers were some of the major activities of ancient hermits.

bed. To him, mountain-and-water painting was consummate because it was a condensation of all natural scenery. The beauty of such famous mountains as the Songshan and Huashan mountains could be expressed in one painting. This theory of his had an important impact on the development of Chinese garden art.

3. The Life of Hermits and their Ideology

Hermits often had their own circles. Several hermits would form a group to keep one another company on travels. There were many famous hermit groups over the centuries, such as the "seven worthies in the bamboo forest" of the Jin Dynasty, the "six solitaries by the bamboo stream" of the Tang Dynasty, the "three dignitaries in the Huashan Mountains" of the Five Dynasties (907-960), and the "friends in the South Mountains". They would sit together and talk, compose poems, paint, read, play chess and musical instruments, drink tea or wine, go fishing, gather herbs in mountains and travel far and wide. All such activities gradually developed into the essential constituents of the private garden. The most famous group of hermit scholars in history was a group of forty-two members headed by Wang Xizhi, a retired scholar of the landed gentry class, who lived during the East Jin Dynasty (317-420). On March 3, in the 9th year of the reign of Emperor Mudi, they gathered at Lan Ting (Orchid Pavilion) in Kuaiji, Zhejiang Province, to celebrate the traditional holiday. They placed delicate blue chinaware wine cups on a winding stream and let them flow with the current. The person in front of whom a cup stopped should drink the wine and compose a poem. This came to be referred to as "flowing cups on a winding stream", and the Preface to the Lan Ting Collection written by Wang Xizhi to record this grand occasion became one of the famous essays in Chinese literature. Men of letters in later ages retained this tradition, and the flowing cup pavilion, built especially in imperial gardens, was a result of its influence on garden architecture. Intricate grooves were chiselled into the stone slab flooring of a pavilion, and water conducted along them. When banquets were given, guests would place wine cups on the water and let them float along.

Liushuiyin, Nanhai, Beijing

Located on the north bank of Nanhai, this pavilion was referred to in the Ming Dynasty as the flowing-cup pavilion. Square in plan, it has a pyramidal roof of glazed tiles. In Qing times, water was conducted into the pavilion, and its name Liushuiyin (Pavilion of the Sound of Flowing Water) was written in Emperor Qianlong's handwriting.

Those in front of whom the wine cups stopped were asked to drink the wine and compose a poem. The Liushuiying (Sound of Flowing Water Pavilion) in Nanhai (South Sea) and Yigan Ting (Beautiful Jade Pearl Pavilion) in the Tanzhesi Temple in Beijing are examples of such pavilions. Zuoshi Linliu (Sitting on a Stone by the Side of a Stream), a scenic spot in the Yuanmingyuan Garden in Beijing, was another type. There was no pavilion, but only a winding groove on the ground.

In feudal China, men of letters were generally Confucianists as long as they were experiencing success, but turned to Taoist philosophy when failure had to be faced. Practically all hermits were Taoists. Ruan Ji, the famous Jin scholar and a member of the "seven worthies in the bamboo forest", and the great scholar Sun Chuo were both believers in Taoism. Wang Xizhi roamed the wild mountains with Taoist priests to gather medicinal herbs, for in those days people believed that fairies and magic herbs could bring men everlasting life.

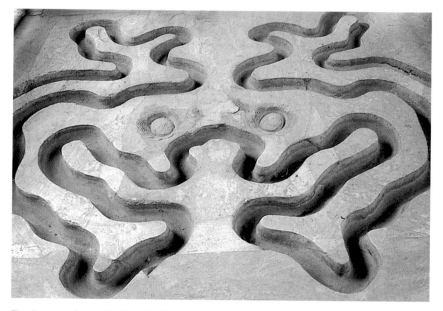

Flowing-cup channel in Yigan Pavilion, Tanzhesi Temple, Beijing

Yigan Pavilion, also known as the flowing-cup pavilion, is in the eastern courtyard of Tanzhesi Temple. The groove for flowing the wine cups is carved on the white marble slab on the floor of the pavilion. The pattern resembles the head of a tiger when viewed from one side, but like a coiled-up dragon when viewed from the opposite one. The pavilion was built according to the ancient tradition of "flowing cups on a winding river".

To be able to see why private gardens developed the way they did, it is essential to understand both the social conditions that led to the emergence of the hermit in China, as well as his way of life and the underlying philosophy.

II. Wei, Jin and the Southern and Northern Dynasties

In this period, hermitage in a natural environment gradually evolved into hermitage in man-made surroundings.

1. Manors

The landed gentry class which had began to emerge towards the end of the Western Han Dynasty (206 B,C.-8 A.D.) became quite influential by the time of the Wei (220-265) and Jin (265-420) period. Manors of famous and powerful families occupied large areas of land, where they could make use of the forests, lakes and ponds, keep herds of sheep and cattle, and battalions of servants. These families were not only in a position to amass great wealth, but practically monopolized cultural development as well. At a time when love of nature and seeking refuge away from the busy world had become a popular social trend, these families began to build their manors in some beautiful locations away from cities to which they could retire, as indeed they did, in times of political turmoil. The manors were practically self-sufficient, and could furnish all the daily necessities. Moreover, their beautiful surroundings also provided an ideal environment for their owners to enjoy themselves.

According to historical records, Shi Chong, a government official at the time of the Western Jin Dynasty (265-316) had a manor in Henan called Jingu Yuan (Golden Grain Garden). There were dense forests and crystal clear springs, and ten hectares of fertile land. Another example of a manor was the mountain villa built by Xie Linyun in Kuaiji, Zhejiang Province. The Xie family was a wealthy and influential family during the East Jin Dynasty (317-420). A detailed description of this manor was given in Xie Linyun's Ode to A Mountain Dwelling. Located in an environment of supreme natural beauty, it was surrounded by forests and fields, with mountains rising both nearby and in the distance. The owner had temples and alters built on his land for Buddhist monks. His own residence occupied only a small area and was surrounded by hills and water. There was a view over to the distant mountains from the south-facing windows, and to the nearby fields from those facing east. Man-made hills and lakes had obviously not yet emerged, but it had already become a major principle to select an idyllic natural environment for residential purposes.

2. Early Private Gardens

It was in the 5th and 6th centuries that the private garden began to emerge. From the time of the Southern Dynasty, there began to appear records of building artificial hills and providing stretches of water adjacent to residences. A famous scholar by the name of Dai Yong who lived during the Southern and Northern dynasties led a hermit's life at Tonglu (Zhejiang Province) with his brother Dai Bo. After Dai Bo died, Dai Yong travelled to Wu (now Suzhou in Jiangsu Province), and started to build a residence together with his scholar friends. They "gathered stones and conducted water, planted trees and dug ditches. Before long the trees grew profusely, and the environment they had constructed looked very much like natural surroundings." This record marked the beginning of building rockeries and providing water to simulate natural scenery. There were other records relating how Prince Wenhui of the State of Ji laid out his Xuanpu Garden, setting it out with many interestingly shaped stones, and how the famous scholar Jiang Yan lived a secluded life in his own garden.

On the whole, the idea of hermitage underwent a course of transformation during this period. Earlier on, hermits had retreated into the wilderness to escape from worldly cares, and to gather magical herbs for eternal life. Now, however, instead of a natural wilderness, residence in an ambiance of man-made hills and water began to be considered an ideal environment for withdrawal from the world, marking the first step towards the simulation of natural scenery in private gardens.

III. Private Gardens of the Tang Dynasty

The period from the Southern and Northern dynasties to the Tang Dynasty saw the decline of the hereditary aristocratic class, and the rise of scholars from the lower classes. It was the introduction of the feudal examination system that brought about this momentous change in the social status of the two types of men of letters. Through an examination procedure carried out on different levels, it was now possible for ambitious commoners to gain higher social status, and even to become high-ranking government officials. This standing

Autumn Voyage with Chrysanthemums in the Boat; section of a painting by Qian Du, Qing Dynasty

Qian Du was a landscape painter, who was praised for his skill in "painting Song style landscapes with Yuan style artistry". The mountains and river in the autumn season, the trees and rustic houses and the small boat on the water depicted in the painting represent the type of natural landscape admired by men of letters in early ages.

once attained, they followed the tradition of building gardens for their own enjoyment. Those of less financial means tended to have smaller gardens laid out near their residences where rockeries, ponds and streams were built to simulate natural scenery, a custom which was eventually to lead to the way the private garden would develop. During this period, large manors and small-scale mountain residences co-existed; there were the large gardens of government officials in cities as well as the pastoral villas in the outskirts.

It was during the Tang Dynasty that poetry and painting flourished in an unprecedented manner, and this had an influence on the art of garden building. It was in this period that sentiments expressed in poetry and concepts in paintings began to be drawn into the creation of gardens because practically all the owners were either poets or painters. The garden of the literati was often seen as an extension of literati painting, whereas the studio school of painting was seen as being expressed in the imperial garden.

The private garden of Pei Du　Pei Du (765-839) was a prime minister during the Tang Dynasty. He had a private garden in the city of Luoyang, and, according to historical records, it was on a grand scale. Its layout was centered on a lake, around which trees and bamboo grew in profusion. In the center of the lake was an island, called Cherry Flower Island, on which stood Shuixin Ting (Pavilion in the Heart of Water). At the southern end of the lake was a stone bridge, and to the east another island Chenguang Dao (Island in Morning Glow). Rockeries stood to the west of the lake, and on the northern side were the main buildings of the garden, richly planted with trees and flowers.

Pingquan Villa The large private resort of the Tang prime minister Li Deyu was located to the west of the Longmen Mountains near Luoyang, Henan Province. On purchasing this old garden from a Qiao family, Li Deyu had mansions, terraces and pavilions built, and had rare trees and interesting rocks brought from the south to be put in the garden. One of the stones was especially famous. Once Li was drunk and slept on the stone. To his surprise, it quickly dispelled the effects of the alcohol, and hence the stone came to be known as "Sober-up Stone".

Wangchuan Resort The most famous private mountain villa or resort of the Tang Dynasty was the Wangchuan Resort of Wang Wei (701-761). Wang Wei was a great poet and painter, and at the same time a high-ranking government official. After resigning from officialdom, he lived a reclusive life at Wangchuan Resort, which was located at an exceptionally beautiful scenic spot in Lantian, Shaanxi Province.

Lonely Dwelling at the Foot of Mountains; section of a painting by Wu Li, Qing Dynasty

The ink-and-wash paintings of Wu Li convey an impression of subdued refinement and high moral integrity. This painting is a good portrayal of the leisurely and peaceful life of hermits in nature's lap.

Living in Leisure; section of a painting by Yao Tingmei, Yuan Dynasty

Yao Tingmei depicted in this painting a pastoral scene away from worldly cares. The mountains, valleys and stream, the rustic thatched cottage, and the hermit living in recluse, such was the ideal realm sought after by men of letters in ancient times.

According to the descriptions in Wang Wei's Collection of Wangchuan, the resort was located in the Wangchuan valley. With the artistic taste of a great poet and painter, it was developed into an idyllic resort, combining natural and man-made scenery. Wang Wei wrote poems to describe some of the scenic spots on his property, introducing the tradition of mixing poetic sentiments and garden scenery.

Thatched cottage in Lushan Mountains Like the Wangchuan Resort of Wang Wei, the poet Bai Juyi also had his cottage built at a famous scenic spot in the Lushan Mountains (Jiangxi Province), but on a smaller scale. In one of his essays, Bai Juyi wrote that when he saw the cloud-veiled mountain peaks and waterfalls, he could not bring himself to leave the place, and so had his thatched cottage built there. It had only three bays, simple and unadorned, with paper screening for windows and bamboo curtains. In front of the house there was a large piece of flat land where a pond was dug for breeding fish. Further to the south was a mountain brook flowing along in the deep shade of ancient pines. To the east of the cottage, a waterfall could be seen, which, in the dimness, resembled a long piece of white silk hanging down, it seemed, from heaven. To the west, bamboos cut in half were installed on the mountain slope to conduct spring water, so that it made a tinkling sound as it flowed down.

IV. Advancing towards the Exquisite Private Gardens of the Northern and Southern Song Dynasties

Buildings in Song Dynasty gardens were generally of moderate size, refined, and in no way gaudy. Unlike the Ming and Qing dynasty buildings, those in Song Dynasty gardens occupied only a comparatively small part of the total area. They were built either on the top of hills to enable a panoramic view to be had, or by the waterside so that pleasure could be gained from the reverted images in the water. They might be built facing flower beds and trees, or set against the side of stones, but on the whole, buildings only played a subsidiary role. It was the natural environment that was given primary consideration in a garden of the literati.

1. Northern Song Dynasty Gardens (960-1127)

After more than fifty years of war and social chaos at the end of the Tang Dynasty, the Northern Song Dynasty brought about a period of peace, and with

Section of a landscape painting by Qian Du, Qing Dynasty

Qian Du traditionally paid great attention to the overall planning of his paintings. The courtyards, houses, pavilions and towers as well as the flowing stream and the small bridge in this painting were all planned with careful deliberation. This was the kind of layout that often served as a model for garden building.

Section of a landscape painting by Wang Yuanqi, Qing Dynasty

This painting by Wang Yuanqi has a strong and powerful style, and compact layout. The running stream, the tiny bridge over the water, and the rustic houses half hidden amid trees in the mountains represent the natural environment aspired to by garden builders.

it came social and economic development. The ruling class encouraged literary pursuits, and consequently ushered in an era which saw literature, painting and philosophy flourish as never before. As a result, the art of garden building matured. Gardens became more exquisite and refined, and the poetry-and-painting motif was carried to new heights. These changes even had an impact on the development of imperial gardens. The Genyue Garden of Emperor Huizong who reigned towards the end of the Northern Song Dynasty clearly showed such an impact, as was mentioned in Imperial Gardens, an earlier volume in this series.

Since the population in cities was growing, and land was becoming more precious, private gardens were generally built on a small scale. It was now the primary aim of the garden builder to have every conceivable type of beautiful scenery condensed into a small garden. As recorded in Records on Famous Gardens in Luoyang, the most famous gardens in Luoyang at that time were the Dule Garden and the private garden of Fu Bic.

Dule Garden This was the private garden of the famous prime minister Sima Guang, who served during the reign of Emperor Zhezong (1086-1100). Located in the city of Luoyang, the garden was not for residential purposes, but solely for enjoyment, and was only of moderate size. Bamboos were planted all over this area, bamboo in China being a symbol of high moral integrity. This was the place where Sima Guang often invited his friends to enjoy the cool in summer time. In addition, there was a terrace in the garden called Jianshan Tai

(Terrace with a View of the Mountain), and on it stood a hall bearing the name of Jianshan Tang (Hall with a View of the Mountain). At the time it was held that it was good for a house to have before it a view of a mountain.

The private garden of Fu Bie Fu Bie was also a prime minister, and served during the reign of both Emperor Renzong (1023-1063) and Emperor Shenzong (1068-1085). His garden was another famous private garden in the city of Luoyang. Built to the east of the residence, it was also centered on a lake. The layout, buildings therein, trees and flowers were all planned with great deliberation.

2. Southern Song Dynasty Gardens (1127-1279)

After Emperor Huizong was captured by invaders from the north, Emperor Gaozong moved the capital to Lin'an (now Hangzhou, Zhejiang Province), and the period from then on came to be called the Southern Song Dynasty. The land to the south of the Yangtze River was fertile and plentiful, and Lin'an was famous for its beautiful West Lake and the surrounding hills. Once the capital, it became the chosen location of high-ranking government officials as well as for men of letters for their gardens. Cities in the vicinity such as Wuxing (now Wuzhou) and Shaoxing also became famous for their private gardens.

The city of Lin'an alone could boast more than a hundred such gardens. One of the most famous was the Nanyuan (South Garden) of the Han family. Han Shizhong was an eminent general, who fought against the Jin invaders from the north. The beauty of the garden was described in Records of the Dreamland and also in Records of the South Garden by the famous scholar Lu You, "The pavilions were all of different styles; no two looked the same. They were so exquisitely built that they seemed to be the work of Master Lu Ban himself. The shooting grounds, the way for horse riding, the winding stream for flowing cups, the intricate grottos in the artificial hills, the magnificent halls, and the rustic huts..... One would be drawn on by all these scenic spots, and would never feel tired of looking at them."

Significant progress was made during the Northern and Southern Song dynasties in the art of building rockeries, handling water, planting trees and constructing diverse types of buildings. Rockeries were built in a great variety of shapes and given different contours. Hillocks, deep valleys and cliffs were henceforth to be found in gardens. The isolated placement of stones began to be popularly adopted. Advances were also made in the treatment of embankments, such as putting up waterside pavilions, building bridges over the water, piling stones up by the lakeside or placing stones to stretch out into the

Sudden Rain over River and Mountains; section of a painting by Tang Yin, Ming Dynasty

Tang Yin's paintings have a free and easy style. In this one, the sudden squall is well depicted, and the painting presents the kind of elegance and refinement pursued by men of letters in their gardens.

water. A wider variety of trees were now used for dense planting to achieve a more exuberant effect. It was altogether a period which saw the private garden maturing at a fast rate.

V. Private Gardens of the Yuan and Ming Dynasties
—— An Artistic Expression of Philosophical Conceptions

Painting as an artistic expression of philosophical conceptions matured during the Yuan and Ming dynasties, and the aesthetic standards of men of letters underwent a significant change during this period. As a result, the private garden was subject to a change in style, which continued till the Qing Dynasty, when the art of garden building reached its zenith.

1. Yuan Dynasty (1271-1368)

With the establishment of the Yuan Dynasty, the social standing of the literati declined dramatically, and they were almost reduced to the position of beggars. As a result, the development of the private garden came to standstill. Since there was no chance of their attaining an official position, scholars began to turn to art, and especially to painting, for their own amusement. The conceptual beauty expressed in their paintings gradually came to be extended to the art of garden building, and gardens began to attain a picture-like style. Huang Gongwang's paintings of powerful mountain peaks, Ni Zan's portrayal of peaceful sylvan settings, and the grand view of mountains and water in Wang Meng's paintings all became blueprints for garden building.

There was little record made of the private garden in the Yuan Dynasty. Only a few were known, such as the Lian Zhuang (Lily Villa) of Zhao Mengfu, a descendant of the imperial family of the Song Dynasty, Ni Zan's Qingbi Ge (Chamber in Secluded Quietude) in Wuxi (Jiangsu Province), the villa of the Lu family and the garden of the Jia family in Changshu (Jiangsu province). However, nothing in detail could be found about those gardens. The only Yuan Dynasty garden still in existence today is the Shizilin Garden (Lion Grove Garden) in Suzhou (Jiangsu Province), although it is no longer in its original state.

Shizilin Garden (Lion Grove Garden) This garden was originally part of a temple built in the later years of the Yuan Dynasty by Monk Tianru to commemorate his teacher, who had resided at Shiziyan (Lions' Rock) in the Tianmu Mountains; hence the name of the garden. At one time during the Ming Dynasty it became the private property of a family. In the course of time it declined, and was rebuilt in later years. Both Emperors Kangxi and Qianlong of Qing (1644-1911) visited this garden, and liked it so much that under Oianlong's direction it was used as a model for one of the gardens in the Summer Resort at Chengde.

According to the records, before Monk Tianru started to build the garden he consulted many famous painters of the time, such as Ni Zan and several others. Ni Zan made a painting of the garden, which was handed down to later generations, and Wei Su wrote an essay, the Record of Shizilin. From the painting and the essay, it can be seen that buildings were only sparsely arranged in the garden at the time it was built, and there were earth hills, bamboo groves and stones and rockeries in abundance. No mention was made of grottos in the rockeries. Towards the middle of the Qing Dynasty, the garden was extended towards the west, and began to take on its present shape, with the rockeries being its most dramatic feature. The layout of the garden is centered on a lake, and the rockeries are chiefly located to its southeast. The main buildings in the garden are to the east and north of the lake, and connected by a long roofed walkway. The rockeries in Shizilin Garden were all built of Taihu stones, and were celebrated for their bizarre shapes. The highest of the peaks was named Shizi Feng (Lion's Peak). Grottos in the

Woyun Shi, Shizilin Garden

Located on top of the eastern artificial hill and seen through the grotesquely shaped Taihu rocks, the pavilion Woyun Shi (Chamber Lying in Clouds) has dramatically upturned eaves. The Taihu rocks resemble clouds in the sky, hence the name of the building.

Window scene, Shizilin Garden

A view through a series of open-tracery windows. The depth of the garden is thus made to appear unfathomable.

Flower bed in a courtyard of Yanyu Hall, Shizilin Garden

The flower bed consists of Taihu stones, small stone bamboos and tall stone peaks. Against the high whitewashed wall it becomes an important scenic focal point of the Yanyu Hall. The courtyard is paved in beautiful patterns.

hills all vary, yet are all linked together. Labyrinth-like, a visitor could soon feel he had lost his way. On the top of the rockery stands the Woyun Ting (Pavilion Reposing in Clouds). Yanyu Hall is to the east of the lake, while Hehua Ting (Lotus Flower Hall), Wusong Yuan (Five-Pine Garden), and the Stone Boat are all to its north. On the west side of the expanse of water are Feipu Ting (Flying Waterfall Pavilion) and Wenmei Ge (Asking-the-Plum Pavilion), and to its south stands a pavilion with a stone tablet in it commemorating Wen Tianxiang, the famous prime minister and general who resisted the invaders from the north at the end of the Ming Dynasty. All the buildings from north to south are connected by a covered walkway.

2. Ming Dynasty (1368-1644)

At the beginning of the Ming Dynasty, the government announced restrictions on the building of private gardens. However, with the growth of economy, private gardens once again prospered, and almost all mansions had gardens attached. The rule of the Ming Dynasty was cruel. Scholars had to undergo a severe process of examination before they could succeed in building up a career as an official, and even then were constantly exposed to the danger of being persecuted. Government officials, therefore, generally did not serve for more than eight years. After they had obtained fame and a respectable social status and accumulated some wealth, they would resign from their posts and return to their native land. There they would engage themselves in cultural and

Section

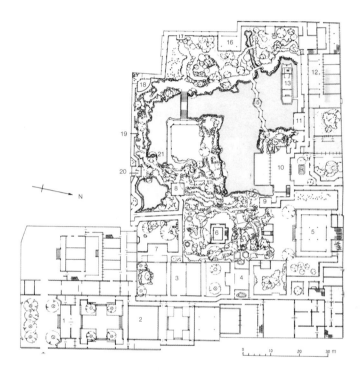

Layout plan

Layout Plan and Section of Shizilin Garden (Lion Grove Garden)

1. Entrance hall	9. Jianshan Lou Storied Building	17. Shuangxiang Xianguan
2. Ancestral temple	10. Meihua Ting Hall	18. Fan-shaped Pavilion
3.Yanyu Hall	11. Zhenqu Ting Pavilion	19. Pavilion with monument in memory
4. Small square hall	12. Anxiang Shuying Lou	of Lord Wen Tianxiang
5. Zhibai Xuan Open Hall	13. Stone boat	20. Pavilion for stone tablet inscribed
6. Woyun Shi	14. Feipu Ting Pavilion	with calligraphy of the emperor
7. Lixue Tang Hall	15. HuxinTing Pavilion	21. Xiao Chibi
8. Xiuzhu Ge Storied Pavilion	16. Wenmei Ge Storied Pavilion	

artistic activities, write books, or set up private schools. To them, garden building was essential for the creation of a cultural environment. This was especially so in the Jiangsu and Zhejiang provinces because to the south of the Yangtze River the land was fertile and people in general were more highly educated. During the Hongwu reign (1368-1398) of the Ming Dynasty, Suzhou already had a population of 2 million, and the grain it delivered annually to the government was as much as one tenth of the nation's total. The city could boast hundreds of scholars who had passed the most advanced level of imperial examination of the Ming and Qing dynasties. This cultural prosperity led to the once again flourishing of the private garden. According to the Local Chronicles of Suzhou, there were more than 270 of them there during the Ming Dynasty. Other cities to the south of the Yangtze River, such as Jinling (now Nanjing), Shanghai, Wuxi, Changshu, Yangzhou and Hangzhou, were all seen as ideal places for scholars or government officers to retire to. Eager to learn, and ready to consult each other, they brought the art of garden building to near perfection.

Garden building in the north of China was mainly carried out in Beijing by rich merchants, high-ranking government officials and aristocrats. Under the influence of imperial gardens, the private ones tended to be gaudy and ostentatious. It was recorded that, "The gardens were mostly built in a grandiose fashion, with too many buildings and lacking a natural environment. One could hardly find a water surface to sail a boat on."

Owing to the growth of the population in cities, the acquisition of land for garden building became increasingly difficult. It was now that the theory of making it possible "to see the limitless in a limited space" became paramount, and the art of creating in a small space scenery that could vie in beauty with the creations of nature herself became an issue of primary concern. In the area to the south of the Yangtze River where garden building had been a popular pastime throughout the Ming Dynasty, many famous garden architects began to emerge, such as Ji Cheng, Zhang Lian and Lu Dieshan. Ji Cheng's book On Garden Building was the most accomplished work of its kind on the subject of private gardens.

Ji Cheng, born in 1582 during the Ming Dynasty, travelled widely in the Jiangsu and Anhui provinces, and specialized in garden building. Being a painter himself, he succeeded in merging the beauty of mountain-and-water paintings into gardens. The gardens he designed, such as the Dongdiyuan Garden in Changzhou, the Wuyuan Garden in Yizhen, and the Shadow Garden in Yangzhou were all famous at the time. His book On Garden Building was a summary of his experiences, and was the only book on the theory of garden-making in ancient China. Some of the basic principles related to the laying out of gardens were first expressed in this book, such as: "gardens, although man-made, should be no less beautiful than the creations of nature herself", "the borrowing of views", and "the art of making clever use of the surroundings and the importance of suiting the garden to the environment". He wrote special chapters on the choice of sites for gardens, buildings in gardens, the construction of rockeries, and the art of borrowing views, and there were many constructional drawings in the book as well. As such, it was an invaluable reference book for garden architects.

The only issue not touched upon was trees and flowers in gardens. The living standard of the literati had, since the Song Dynasty, gradually improved, and the tradition of seeking refuge in the wilds belonged to the past. In addition, the owners of gardens were mostly government officers, who, although resigned from their posts, had become accustomed to living in style. As a result, they tended to have more buildings erected in their gardens to satisfy their personal needs. Trees and flowers could die, but buildings represented property, which could be bequeathed to the following generations. This trend was at its most popular during the Qing Dynasty (1644-1911), the admiration of the beauty of nature giving way to a passionate interest in buildings, which became more elaborate and took on a variety of shapes.

Zhang Lian, born in 1587, was also a famous garden architect during the Ming Dynasty. Being a painter, he was especially good at piling up stones and building rockeries, and applying theories of painting to the building of rockeries. Hengyun Shanzhuang (Mountain Villa Reposing in Clouds) in Songjiang, Zhuting Hushu (Bamboo-Pavilion Lakeside Resort) in Jiaxin, Lejiao Yuan (Garden with Farm Interests), and Foshui Shanzhuang (Brushing-over-Water Mountain Villa) were some of his famous creations. Wang Shiming, the great painter, was full of praise for the artistry of Zhang Lian's rockeries saying, "so exquisite was his artistry that it almost puts the work of nature to shame".

Zhuozhengyuan Garden (Humble Administrator's Garden) Built in the 4th year of the Zhende reign of Ming, this garden goes back almost 500 years. It was first owned by a high-ranking government official Wang Xianchen, who unfortunately was slandered by the court secret agent and was assigned a much lower post as a county magistrate. This explains the name of the garden.

According to Record of Zhuozhengyuan of the Wang Family and Painting on Zhuozhengyuan by the famous scholar painter Wen Zhengming, open and spacious natural scenery was the garden's leitmotif. There was a profusion of trees and attractive expanses of water in the garden, and only a few buildings were dotted about.

During the Qing Dynasty, the garden was redeveloped on several occasions, and extensions were made gradually giving it the shape it has today. It is divided into three sections, the central part, Zhuozhengyuan Garden (the Humble Administrator's Garden), the west part, Buyuan Garden, and the east part, Guitian Yuanju (Residence after Return to the Fields). The central part, which has kept its original name, occupies more than 12,000 square meters,

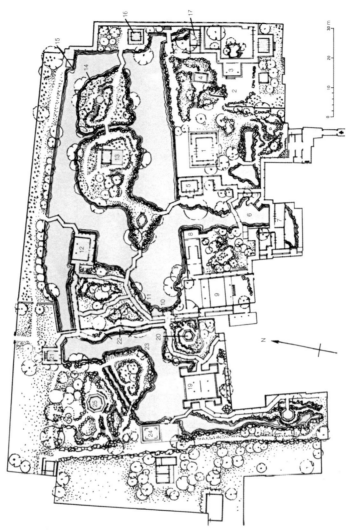

30 m

20

10

0

N

Plan of Zhuozhengyuan Garden

1. Yuanxiang Tang Hall
2. Pipa Yuan Orchid
3. Linglong Guan
4. Xiuqi Ting Pavilion
5. Yiqu Xuan Hall
6. Xiaofeihong
7. Xiaocanglang Water Pavilion
8. Xiangzhou Isle
9. Yulan Tang Hall
10. Bieyou Dongtian
11. Liuyinluqu Wingding path
12. Jianshan Lou Storied Building
13. Xuexiangyunwei Ting Pavilion
14. Beishan Ting Pavilion
15. Luyi Ting Pavilion
16. Wuzhuyouju
17. Haitangchunwu
18. Tingyu Xuan Pavilion
19. Sanshiliu Yuanyang Guan
20. Yiliang Ting Pavilion
21. Daoying Lou Storied Building
22. Waterside roofed walkway
23. Yushuitongzuo Xuan Hall
24. Liuting Ge Storied Building
25. Fucui Ge Storied Building

one third of which being water. According to Wen Zhengming's Record of Zhuozhengyuan of the Wang Family, all the pavilions and terraces were built low by the waterside, and bridges were constructed of flat stone slabs hugging the surface of the water. The layout was designed to make the water surface look more extensive than it actually was. To the south of the lake stands the main building of the garden, Yuanxiang Tang (Hall of Distant Fragrance). Being a four-sided hall, the scenery can be enjoyed in every direction. The Linshui Yuetai (Moon Terrace by Waterside) at the back of the hall facing north is an ideal place for enjoying lotus flowers on summer days. The group of buildings on the southern side of the lake consisting of the flowery hall Yulan Tang (Magnolia Hall), the land boat Xiangzhou (Fragrant Isle) and the corridor bridge Xiaofeihong (Little Flying Rainbow), form the highlight of the garden. Pipa Yuan (Loquat Orchad) is an independent courtyard separated from the rest of the garden by an undulating wall. The buildings in the courtyard comprise

Mingse Lou, Liuyuan Garden / opposite page

Located on the southern bank of the lake, Mingse
Lou (Bright Zither Storied Building) is one of the
main buildings in the garden. It connects with Hanbi
Shanfang (Cold Emerald Green Mountain Villa) on its
west side. The difference in height of the two buildings
makes for an attractive sight.

Guanyun Feng, Liuyuan Garden

The largest single Taihu rock in the Suzhou gardens,
Guanyun Feng (Cloud-Capped Peak) is located to
the west of Lingquanqishouzhi Guan (House for
the Venerable elderly). Everything around has been
arranged to set off the rock. Tall, slender, perforated
and full of pits and crevices, it is believed to be one of
the rare stones chosen for Emperor Huizong's Genyue
Garden laid out during the Song Dynasty.

Yulinglong, Yuyuan Garden

Standing in front of Yuhua Tang (Jade Flower Hall),
Yulinglong (Exquisite Jade) is a unique Taihu stone,
which has all the attributes required for it to be
considered remarkable: tall, slender, perforated and
full of pits and crevices. It, too, is believed to be a
precious stone intended for the famous Genyue
Garden of Song.

Linglong Guan (Exquisite Jade House), Jiashi Ting (Precious Fruit Pavilion) and
Xiuqi Ting (Beautiful Embroidery Pavilion). Looking through the moon gate
in the undulating wall, the lake, the rockery and the pavilion on its top can be
seen. At the east end of the lake is Wuzhuyouju Ting (Secluded Pavilion amid
Phoenix Trees and Bamboos), which has moon-shaped doors on all four sides.
At the western end of the lake is a winding roofed walkway Liuyinluqu (Willow-
shaded Winding Path) leading to Jianshan Lou (Storied Building with a View of
Mountains) in the north.

The lake in the center of Zhuozhengyuan Garden is of narrow shape, and
contains two small islands, each having a pavilion. At the west end of the lake is
a moon-gate entrance Bieyou Dongtian (Realm of Exceptional Beauty), which
leads to the western section, the Buyuan Garden.

The layout of this section differs entirely from the open, spacious style of
Ming gardens. The arrangement is centered on a zigzag-shaped lake, with the

main building, the Sanshiliu Yuanyang Guan (Thirty-six Mandarin Ducks Hall), on its southern side, used mainly for entertainment. To the north of the lake is a rockery, on which stands Fucui Ge (Floating Jade Storied Pavilion). The lake in the western section is a narrow strip of water running north-south. At its northern end is Daoying Lou (Storied Building with Inverted Reflection in Water), and at its southern end Yiliang Ting (Pavilion for Enjoying Scenery in Two Directions), the two setting off one another. Along the garden wall to the east of the lake is a waterside roofed walkway. It is a light and natural-looking construction, undulating or winding along the water's edge, and forms the highlight of this section of the garden. The buildings in the eastern part, Guitian Yuanju, were all constructed in recent years.

Liuyuan Garden (Lingering Garden) This is a garden celebrated for its rare stones. When first built during the Jiajing reign (1522-1566) of Ming, it was named Dong Yuan (East Garden). It was devastated towards the end of the Ming Dynasty, then renamed Hanbi Shanzhuang (Cold Emerald Green Mountain Villa), and later, Liuyuan Garden (Lingering Garden) after redevelopment during the Qing Dynasty. In the Confucian scholar Yu Yue's Record of Liu Yuan, the author praised the garden's beauty: "The uniqueness of its springs and stones, the beauty of its flowers and trees, and the concealed and tranquil location of its pavilions and verandas, so remarkable is the elegance of the garden that it is unparallelled among all the famous gardens in the city of Suzhou". The garden which we see today is based on the plan of Hanbi Shanzhuang.

The lake lies in the middle of the central section, and rockeries stand to its north and west. The main buildings, Hanbi Shanfang (Cold Emerald Green Mountain Lounge) and Mingse Lou (Bright Zither Storied Hall) on the southern side of the lake were still arranged in the Ming style. On top of the rockery on the northern bank of the lake is Ke Ting Pavilion, and to the west is a pavilion named Wenmuxixiang Xuan (Veranda for Smelling the Fragrance of Sweet-Scented Osmanthus). On the east side of the lake are Xi Lou (West Storied Building) and Quyu Lou (Intricate Vale Storied Building). The small island in the middle of the stretch of water is called Xiao Penglai (Small Penglai Island). On the east side of the lake there is a peninsula, on which stands the Houpu Pavilion, a zigzag bridge connecting the peninsula and the island.

The building group in the eastern section of the garden was the residential quarter of the owner. The main hall, Wufeng Xianguan (Five-Peak Celestial

Section

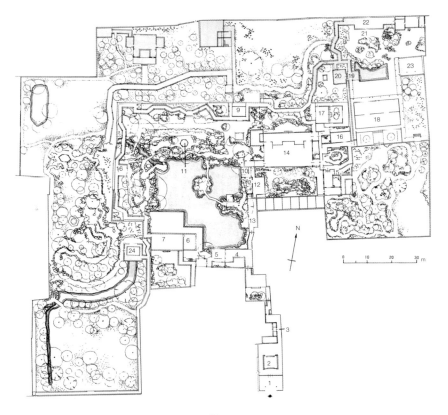

Plan

Plan and Section of Liuyuan Garden (Lingering Garden)

1. Entrance
2. Small yard
3. Winding roofed walkway
4. Gumujiaoke
5. Luyin
6. Mingse lou Storied Building
7. Hanbi Shangfang Hall
8. Wenmuxixiang Xuan Open Pavilion
9. Yuancui Ge Pavilion
10. Qingfengchiguan Guest House
11. Ke Ting Pavilion
12. West Storied Building
13. Quxi Low Storied Building
14. Wufeng Xianguan Hall
15. Shilin Xiaowu
16. Yifeng Xuan Pavilion
17. Huanwo Dushu Study
18. Linquanqishouzhi Guan Hall
19. Guanyun Tai Platform
20. Jiaqing Xiyu Kuaixuezhi Ting Pavilion
21. Guanyun Feng Rock
22. Guanyun Low Storied Building
23. Daiyun Hut
24. Huopopo Di

Hall), is built of precious Nanmu wood, and to its east is a mandarin-duck hall, Linquanqishuozhi Guan (Hall for the Venerable Elderly). In the yard to the north stands the famous Taihu rockery Guanyun Feng (Cloud-Capped Peak), rising to a height of 6.5 meters. The most outstanding feature of Liuyuan Garden is its intricate spatial quality. Spaces, large and small, bright and dark, open and secluded, are interwoven to form contrasts, and to offset each other. Movement through the design is controlled and directed in a series of planned visual experiences. Open tracery windows of diverse forms and shapes, adding greater depth and charm to the scenery, constitute another special feature of the garden.

Yuyuan Garden (Happy Garden) Located in Shanghai, this garden was first built in the 38th year of the Jiajing reign of Ming (1559) by a government official Pan Yunduan. As the name of the garden suggests, Pan had the garden built to bring happiness to his aged parents. It covered an area of over 4.6

Dachang Tai, Yuyuan Garden

Standing to the south of Dianchun Tang, north of Hexu Tang and west of Kuai Low, Dachang Tai (Storied Pavilion for Singing and Playing Musical Instruments) is an important building in the northeastern section of the garden, a place for musical performances. The dramatically upturned eaves are of exquisite design.

hectares, and was known at the time as "the crown of all famous gardens in the southeast area". The most specific feature in Yuyuan Garden is its grand rockery hill, a rare piece of work by the famous rockery builder Zhang Nanyang. Rising up to 12 meters, the hill has range upon range of peaks and cliffs, and steps through the rocks leading intricately up to the top. "To look at it from afar, one would never believe it was made by man." A lake lies to its south, and on the southern side of the lake is a two-storied building. Lying again to its south is the main building of the garden, Sansui Tang (Hall of Three Spikes of Grain), which was rebuilt during the reign of Emperor Qianlong of Qing on the basis of Leshou Tang (Hall of Happy Longevity) dating from the Ming times. Patterns of spikes of grain, vegetables and fruit were carved in relief on the window frames of this hall to symbolize a rich harvest. The winding roofed walkway to the east of the grand rockery hill is called Jianru Jiajing (Leading Gradually into a Splendid Realm). Further east, there are small courtyards consisting of various groups of buildings, including Yule Xie (Happy Fish Waterside Pavilion) and Wanhua Lou (Storied Building with Thousands of Flowers). To the east of Wanhua Lou, there are two rows of courtyards arranged on a central axis, and to its south is another group of buildings comprising of Jiushi Xuan (Nine Lion Pavilion), Yuhua Tang (Jade Flower Hall), and a pond. In front of the hall stands a huge Taihu rock called Yulinglong (Exquisite Jade) which, as the story goes, was a piece of rock chosen for the Genyue Garden of Emperor Huizong of the Song Dynasty, but somehow went astray.

Zhanyuan Garden (Looking-into-the-Distance Garden) Located in Nanjing, this garden was first built in the early years of the Ming Dynasty, and was the garden home of Xu Da, the Prince of Zhongshan. It underwent many changes in the course of time. When Emperor Qianlong of Qing travelled to the south, he visited the garden twice. Yuan Jiang, a famous painter, made a painting of the garden, which was handed down from generation to generation. It proved a valuable source of information, showing for example that the Zhanyuan Garden possessed impressive rockeries and rocks. The Zhanyuan Garden of today was rebuilt on the basis of the original layout. There are two rockeries in the garden, one in the south, and the other in the north. In the western part of the garden, there is another hill piled with earth. A substantial part of the northern rockery dates from the early Ming period, and consists of grottos, steep cliffs and projecting precipices. It is half-encircled by the lake at its foot, and a bridge of flat stone spans the water, hugging the surface. Trees grow

**Layout Plan of Zhanyuan Garden
(Looking-into-distance Garden)**

1. Entrance
2. Flowery Hall
3. Jingmiao Tang
4. Newly built artificial hill
5. Waterside pavilion
6. Old rockery
7. Newly built area

Layout Plan of Jichangyuan Garden (Garden to The Heart's Content)

1. Entrance
2. Shuangxiao Ci Temple
3. Bingli Ci Hall
4. Hanzhen Zhai Study
5. Jiushi Tai
6. Jiashu Tang Hall
7. Hanbi Ting Pavilion
8. Qixing Qiao Bridge
9. Bayi Jian
10. Hebutan
11. Qingxiang Yuedong
12. Zhiyu Jian
13. Yupan Ting Pavilion
14. Jinhuiyi Lake

abundantly all over the hill and, in the shade of the trees, intricate paths lead up the hill, and bridges cross dangerous-looking valleys and lead over cliffs. The main building in the garden, Jingmiao Tang (Hall of Superb Quietude), stands to the south of the North Hill, facing the lake to its south. On the southern shore of the lake is the South Hill, rebuilt in later years.

Other Ming Dynasty Gardens In addition to those mentioned above, there are many more private gardens from the Ming era in the area to the south of the Yangtze River. However, they were mostly rebuilt during the Qing period, or even later, and so cannot be regarded as genuine Ming creations. For example, Fenggu Xingwo (Travelling Resort in Phoenix Valley) in Wuxi (Jiangsu Province) was first built during the Zhende reign of Ming as the private garden of Qing Jin, the defense minister. Its name was changed to Jichangyuan Garden (Garden to the Heart's Content) during the Qing Dynasty. Both Emperors Kangxi and Qianlong of Qing visited the garden several times. The latter liked it so much that he had the Garden of Harmonious Interest built in the Summer Palace in Beijing modelled on it. There were other gardens such as Xiaoyuan Garden in Songjiang, Nanyuan Garden (South Garden) and Yanyuan Garden (Sheltered Garden) in Taicang, Tanyuan Garden (Sandalwood Garden), Yiyuan Garden (Garden of Beautiful Ripples) and Sanlaoyuan Garden (Garden of Three Old Folks) in Nanxiang, and Laihe Zhuang (Villa where Cranes Come), Qingshan Zhuang (Villa in Blue Mountains) and Guileyuan Garden (Garden for Happy Return) in Changzhou. The famous garden architect Ji Cheng, who lived at the end of the Ming Dynasty, created many fine gardens including the Yingyuan Garden (Shadow Garden) in Yangzhou, Dongdiyuan Garden in Changzhou, and Wuyuan Garden (Awakening Garden) in Yizhen. They were all famous at the time.

Gardens in Beijing Practically all gardens in the north of China were in Beijing. Private gardens mainly belonged to aristocratic families and rich merchants. Their somewhat philistine taste often led to their gardens being generally ostentatious and almost vulgar. Some of the famous gardens were the Qinghuayuan Garden (Clear and Beautiful Garden) of Li Wei, the Shaoyuan Garden (Spoon Garden) of Mi Wanzhong, and the Wanyuan Garden of Li Qi. These gardens were all located in today's Haidian district in the northwestern suburb of Beijing. Shaoyuan Garden in due time became the campus of Yanjing University (now Peking University). Wanyuan Garden had a circumference of nearly 10 kilometers. The main building was Yihai Hall. There was a large lake planted with lotus flowers. From there the undulating hills in the distance could clearly be seen. The garden was richly planted with gigantic trees, bamboo and flowers, and there were countless rare stones. It was later amalgamated into the boundaries of an imperial garden.

Summing up, the private gardens of the Ming period were a further development of the Song and Yuan gardens. Natural beauty remained the theme, although changes were inevitable to cope with the growth of population and the fact that there was less land for garden building. The lakes and rockeries tended to be reduced in size and took on a more symbolic character compared with those in earlier gardens. The layout design generally had the lake in the center, with the rockeries to its north and the main buildings to its south, thus enabling all the scenery to be enjoyed. The rockeries of the time usually had gentle contours, and were mostly built with a mixture of stones and earth, so as to facilitate the planting of trees. The expanses of water were always arranged in a concentrated manner, but with small bays and nooks to make the lake look natural. The architecture of the buildings had greatly advanced, a great variety of buildings now being constructed such as halls, studies, guest houses, pavilions, storied buildings, waterside pavilions, terraces and roofed walkways. There were even special chambers for playing musical instruments, or for drinking tea, and stone tables and stools were used for outdoor activities. The book On Garden Building written towards the end of the Ming period was an illustration of how the art of garden building had prospered, and of the advances in theory and practice.

VI. Private Gardens of the Qing Dynasty
—— The Architecture of Buildings Moving into the Foreground

The reign of Emperors Kangxi (1662-1722) and Qianlong (1736-1795) of the Qing Dynasty (1644-1911) was a period of strong economic growth and national solidarity. In the area to the south of the Yangtze River, the weather was mild and the land fertile. It was a part of China that could boast a high cultural development. Ever since the Song and Ming days, there had been a tradition of building private gardens in the region, and this passion was nurtured by the fact that the emperors too took a strong interest in garden building.

In as early as the reign of Emperor Shunzhi, the first of the Qing Dynasty, regulations concerning the building of residences for government officials and aristocrats of different ranks and status were promulgated by the government. There were restrictions on the dimension of the residences, the colour and shape of the roofs, doors and columns, the height of the podiums, and the styles of the paintings. Gardens were the only exception. Magnificent gardens, therefore, could be found practically in all the aristocratic residences in Beijing. These gardens, almost without exception, were large in size, and had a great number of halls, storied buildings, terraces, pavilions, lakes and hills, and flowers and trees. Yet, under the influence of the imperial gardens, they were all luxurious and grandiose, and were in no way imbued with the refined taste of the private gardens to be found in the south of the country.

Chengzeyuan Garden Located in today's western district of Beijing, this was a garden attached to the residence of Prince Guo of the Qing Dynasty. According to the descriptions in the Prologue to Poems on Chengzeyuan, the garden was sited to the east of the residential quarter. There were hills and lakes, pavilions and halls. Some of the scenic spots in the garden were imitations of famous scenic spots in the south of the country. For example, Chunhe Tang (Hall of Spring Harmony), the tower on the island in the center of the lake, was modelled on the Golden Hill Temple of Zhenjiang. Yanyu Ji (Smoke-like Rain Rock), the piece of rock projecting into the lake, was an artificial version of the Yanzi Ji (Swallow Rock) in Nanjing. The other scenic spots included Yungen (Root of Cloud), a stone precipice rising out of the water; Laiqing Xie (Waterside Pavilion Coming out of the Blue), a waterside pavilion for enjoying the scenery; Lanyun Tai (Cloud Embracing Terrace), a platform for enjoying the moon; Xiao Taoyuan (Lesser Land of Peach Blossom), an area planted with a mixture of peaches and pines. A study, a lodge among the hills, a Buddhist temple, a bamboo grove, a field for planting vegetables, and a great variety of flowers and grass completed the picture of the garden. Scholars doing research on the famous novel The Dream of Red Mansions held that this garden was the blueprint for the Grand View Garden described in the story.

Garden in Gongwang Fu (Prince Gong's Residence) This garden, now situated to the west of the Shisahai Lake in Beijing, was the garden of an aristocratic residence, and has over the course of time remained well kept. The mansion of Prince Gong was well known in Beijing for its grandeur and elegance. The garden, called Cuijin Yuan (Garden Gathering all Splendours), was located to the north of the residential quarter. The buildings and scenic spots are arranged on three parallel axes. From the south to the north along the central axis are the main garden gate, the Dule Rock, the Fu He (River of Happiness), Anshan Tang (Hall of Peace and Benevolence), a square lake, a grand rockery,

Yaoyue Ting (Hall of Invitation to the Moon), and Fu Dian (Hall of Happiness). Arranged along the eastern axis are the storied building of a theatre and several courtyards. In the front of this group of buildings is a floral-pendant gate, and outside the gate there is a flowing-cup pavilion. The section on the west side begins in the south with a wall resembling a city wall, and linked with a grand rockery. To the north stands an open pavilion, Qiushui Shanfang (Autumn Water Mountain Villa), Miaoxiang Ting (Pavilion of Exquisite Fragrance), and Yizhi Zhai (Study Beneficial to the Mind). At the northernmost end is a large lake with a pavilion in its center. The residence of Prince Gong occupied an area of six hectares, and its layout and design were modelled on the sumptuous style of imperial gardens. It had nothing in common with the private gardens in the southern regions.

Suiyuan Garden In the early years of the Qing Dynasty, there were many private gardens in Nanjing, (Jiangsu Province), among which Suiyuan Garden was the most famous. Located on a piece of land elevated on both the southern and northern sides, but low in the middle, its layout comprised three parallel sections. All the main buildings were arranged on the ridge to the north, while on the southern side, only minor buildings for enjoyment. A mountain stream ran through the middle section. The owner of the garden was Yuan Mei, a celebrated scholar of the time.

This garden, as large as 14.50 hectares, had no walls around it. On beautiful spring and autumn days, people would flock there for recreation. Only a few buildings in the garden were for the exclusive use of the master and not open to the public including Lujin Xuan (Green Dustless Veranda); Xiaocang Shanfang (Xiaocang Mountain Villa), the hall for giving banquets to friends; Xialiang Dong'ao Suo (Cool-in-Summer-and-Warm-in-Winter Study); Luxiao Ge (Dawn-in-the-Green Storied Pavilion) for enjoying the beautiful scenery in the distance, and the library which had a collection of 300,000 volumes. According to Yuan Mei's poems, there were 24 scenic spots in his garden, with flowers all year round. His garden, he said, was a delight even on rainy or snowy days. In feudal times, it was rare that a private garden was open to the public, and Yuan Mei was the first to initiate such a practice. In the latter years of the Qing Dynasty, the garden gradually declined and sank into obscurity.

In the early years of the Qing Dynasty, Yangzhou (Jiangsu Province) was a centre of communication, and a place where rich salt merchants met. The economy prospered, and garden building became popular, even more so after

the Emperors Kangxi and Qianlong had honoured the city with their presence. According to Records on Painted Boats of Yangzhou, more than a hundred private gardens lined the banks of the Slender West Lake, starting from the north city gate and stretching all the way to Pingshan Hall at the foot of Shugang Hillock. Writing about the splendid gardens of Yangzhou, the Qing Dynasty scholar Shen Sanbai said: "Even marble towers and jade houses in the celestial land cannot be more magnificent than what I see here." Tragically, most of the gardens in Yangzhou were ruined in war. Geyuan Garden, Heyuan Garden and Xiaopangu Garden are the only few that have survived.

Geyuan Garden (Bamboo Garden) This garden was built during the Jiaqing reign (1796-1820) of the Qing Dynasty, of which the layout is dominated by Guihua Ting (Osmanthus Hall). From Guihua Ting, the scenes in all directions could be enjoyed. It is well-known for rockery. Four rockery works were constructed of four kinds of stones, representing the four different seasons. The spring rockery was built of stone slabs, summer rockery of Taihu stones, autumn rockery of yellow stones and winter rockery of Xuan stones. The colours and images are quite consistent with the concept. There is a winding pond to the north of Guihua Ting, and a long building of seven bays connecting the summer rockery and autumn rockey.

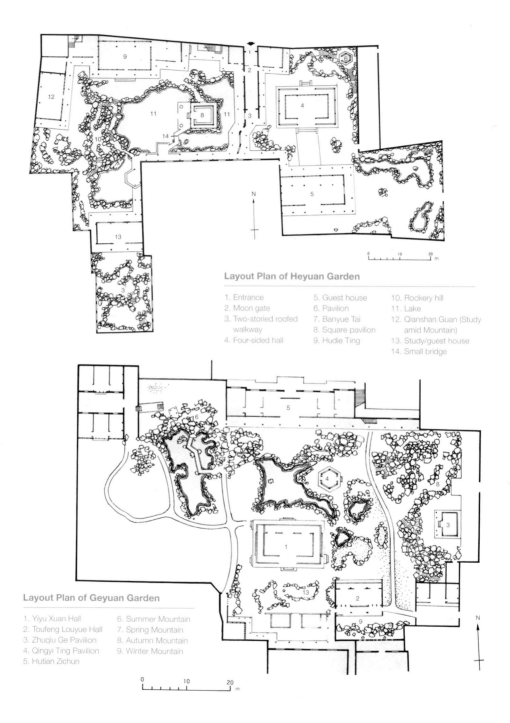

Layout Plan of Heyuan Garden

1. Entrance
2. Moon gate
3. Two-storied roofed walkway
4. Four-sided hall
5. Guest house
6. Pavilion
7. Banyue Tai
8. Square pavilion
9. Hudie Ting
10. Rockery hill
11. Lake
12. Qianshan Guan (Study amid Mountain)
13. Study/guest house
14. Small bridge

Layout Plan of Geyuan Garden

1. Yiyu Xuan Hall
2. Toufeng Louyue Hall
3. Zhuqiu Ge Pavilion
4. Qingyi Ting Pavilion
5. Hutian Zichun
6. Summer Mountain
7. Spring Mountain
8. Autumn Mountain
9. Winter Mountain

Parallel roofed walkway, Heyuan Garden

Located in the western part of the garden, the parallel roofed walkway serves to connect all the buildings round the lake in the center.

Heyuan Garden Laid out during the Guangxu reign (1875-1908) of the Qing Dynasty, the garden is made up of two sections. The residential quarter in the east has a three-bay open pavilion, a four-sided hall, and a rockery built against the wall to the rear of the hall. The garden in the west has a large lake in the center surrounded by storied buildings. On the north shore is a butterfly hall, on the east a square pavilion built over the water, and on the west a rockery. Storied roofed walkways run along the south shore. An outstanding feature of this garden are the walkways, 400 metres in length, that connect the two-storied buildings on the northern and southern sides of the lake.

Xiaopangu Garden Built during the Guangxu reign, this garden used to be the residence of Zhou Fu, governor of Guangdong and Guangxi provinces. On entering the garden, one comes on the east side to a rockery, built entirely of Taihu stones, and a zigzag shaped flowery hall. Behind the hall is a square lake, with a pavilion built over the water. The rockery facing the lake is backed by a wall, and a pavilion stands on its top. A stone bridge crossing the lake joins up the grotto in the rockery. This garden is very small, but is arranged with intricacy, with a variety of buildings and rich plantings of trees and flowers. It is a typical example of private gardens in the late period.

Suzhou in the Qing era continued to attract men of letters as an ideal place to live on retirement. According to the Record of Suzhou Prefecture issued during the Tongzhi reign (1862-1874), more than 130 private gardens were built in the Qing Dynasty alone. It can be said without exaggeration that the Suzhou gardens were the finest in China. A number of these fortunately still exist, and constitute a part of China's precious cultural heritage.

Wangshiyuan Garden (Retired Fisherman's Garden) This garden was first built during the Southern Song Dynasty (1127-1279) on the deserted site of Wanjuan Tang (Hall of Ten Thousand Books), and was named Yuyin (Fisherman's Hermitage). When it was rebuilt by Song Zongyuan during the reign of Emperor Qianlong (1736-1795) of Qing, he kept the meaning of the original name and called it the Retired Fisherman's Garden.

The garden is made up of three sections, the residential quarter in the east, the main garden in the centre, and the inner garden in the west. The living quarters are arranged on a north-south central axis, starting with the sedan-chair hall, the main hall, and the inner hall. To the rear of the inner hall, there is a small open pavilion called Tiyun Shi (Serried Clouds Chamber), which now serves as the main entrance to the garden. The main garden has a lake in its center, and all the buildings are arranged round it. The group of buildings to the south of the lake include Xiaoshan Conggui Xuan (Hall of Sweet Osmanthus Hillock) , Daohe Guan (House of Peace) and the chamber for playing the zither. This group of buildings was where the owner of the garden entertained his guests. The buildings for studying and painting were arranged to the north of the lake, including Wufeng Shuwu (Five-Peaks Study), Jixu Zhai (Study of the Ethereal) and Kansongduhua Xuan (Veranda for Enjoying Pine Trees and Deriving Joy from Paintings). A high wall stands near the living quarters on the east side of the lake. Here there is a rockery and an abundance of trees and

Dianchunyi, Wangshiyuan Garden

In the courtyard of Dianchunyi (Late Spring Study) there used to be an abundance of herbaceous peony, which flowers in late spring; hence the name of the study. The courtyard is simple and refined, and the beautiful paving further enhances its charm.

flowers. The inner garden is a secluded area on the west side of the lake. The main building in this quarter is Dianchun Yi (Late Spring Study), an exquisite two-bay study. Bamboos and banana trees grow behind, and stones add a decorative touch. When viewed through the north window of the study, it is as if one is looking at a picture. The Chinese-style garden Ming Xuan built in the Metropolitan Museum in New York in 1980 was modelled on this garden.

Yiyuan Garden (Delightful Garden) Built during the Guangxu reign of the late Qing Dynasty, this was the private garden of Gu Wenbin. It is divided into the east and west garden areas by a parallel roofed walkway. The eastern part was formerly the site of the residence of a Ming Dynasty minister, whereas the western garden area is an extension made by Gu Wenbin. Since it was built later than many other gardens, its architect was able to draw on the merits of earlier gardens, thus creating a distinctive and delightful landscape environment. The eastern part of the garden consists of several courtyards, the main building being a four-sided hall called Baishi Xuan (Veranda in Honour of Stones). To its north stands Poxian Qinguan (Celestial Zither House). Several curiously shaped stones are placed outside the north window as a decorative feature framed by the window. Sishi Xiaosa Ting (Restful in all Four Seasons Pavilion), Yuyan Ting (Pavilion of Continuous Jade), Yuhong Ting (Jade Rainbow Pavilion) and Shifang (Stone Boat) are some of the other buildings in this group. The garden sector is in the west. The lake is long and narrow, and rockeries with grottos and a pavilion on top are set out to its north. The main building on the southern bank of the lake is a mandarin-duck hall, one half bearing the name of Ouxiang Xie (Fragrant Lotus Root Waterside Pavilion) and the other Chuyue Xuan (Moon-Ploughing Veranda). The tables and chairs in Ouxiang Xie are made of the roots of old trees, exquisite and refined in taste. To the west of the waterside pavilion, there are two pavilions, Biwu Qifeng (Green Parasol Trees where Phoenix Dwell), and Mianbi Ting (Pavilion Facing the Wall). Further west are Huafang Zhai (Painted Boat Studio) and Zhanlu Zhai (Study of Crystal Clear Dew).

In addition to being small, compact and exquisitely designed, the garden is noted for its couplets, stone slates, Taihu stones, and lacebark pines. The stone slates inlaid into the walls of its roofed walkways are mostly carved with the writings of famous calligraphers of the Jin, Tang, Song, Yuan and Ming dynasties, and are of great cultural value.

Ouyuan Garden (Twin Garden) This was a comparatively large residence and garden covering about 7,600 square meters. It was first built during the

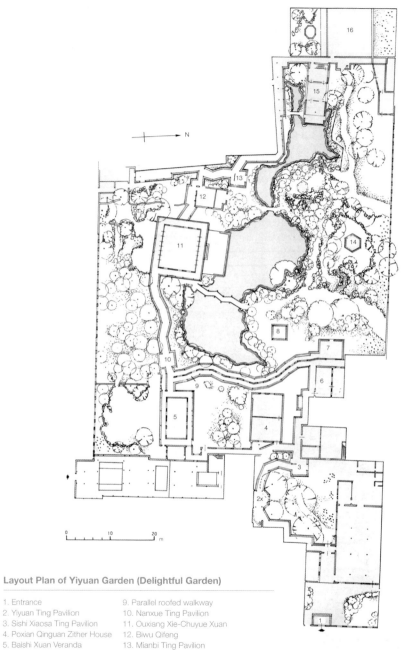

Layout Plan of Yiyuan Garden (Delightful Garden)

1. Entrance
2. Yiyuan Ting Pavilion
3. Sishi Xiaosa Ting Pavilion
4. Poxian Qinguan Zither House
5. Baishi Xuan Veranda
6. Stone Boat
7. Suolu Xuan Veranda
8. Jinsu Ting Pavilion

9. Parallel roofed walkway
10. Nanxue Ting Pavilion
11. Ouxiang Xie-Chuyue Xuan
12. Biwu Qifeng
13. Mianbi Ting Pavilion
14. Xiao Canglangting Pavilion
15. Shufang Zhai Studio
16. Zhanlu Zhai Study

Drawing of the courtyard

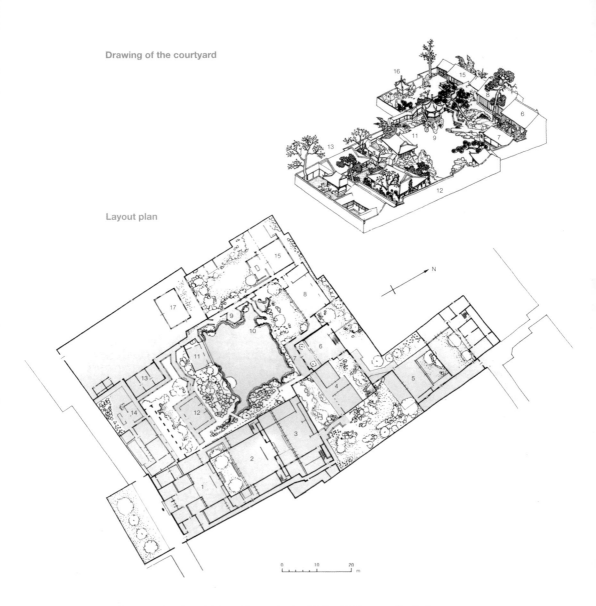

Layout plan

Layout Plan and Drawing of Wangshiyuan Garden (Retired Fisherman Garden)

1. Sedan-chair hall
2. Main ahll
3. Xiexiu Lou Storied Building
4. Wufeng Shuwu Study
5. Tiyun Shi
6. Jixu Zhai Study
7. Zhuwaiyizhi Xuan
8. Kansongduhua Xuan Veranda
9. Yuedaofenglai Ting Pavilion
10. Stone projecting over the water
11. Zhuoying Shuige Waterside Pavilion
12. Xiaoshan Conggui Xuan Hall
13. Daohe Guan
14. Chamber for playing the zither
15. Dianchun Yi Study
16. Lengquan Ting Pavilion
17. Greenhouse

early Qing Dynasty, and was extended in later years under the supervision of a famous painter. The residential quarter consisted of four rows of courtyards, and two gardens were arranged to its east and west, hence the name Twin Garden. The east garden, about 2,500 square meters in area, has a yellow stone rockery at its center. To the east is a long and narrow lake. A waterside pavilion, Shanshuijian (Pavilion amid Hills and Water), spans the water at the southern end of the lake. To the north of the rockery is the main building of the garden, a two-storied hall called Chengqu Caotang (City Corner Thatched Cottage), which is connected with the residence to its west by roofed walkways. On both the western and southern sides of the rockery are winding roofed walkways, which end at Tinglu Lou (Tower for Listening to the Sweep of Oars) in the southeast corner of the garden. The yellow stone rockery is made up of two halves, with a deep valley in-between. The east side facing the lake takes the form of a steep precipice, and has a winding bridge at its foot. It is a representative of the style of rockeries in Suzhou gardens. The west garden is small, and the main building there is a study called Zhilian Laowu (Old House with Woven Curtain). The courtyard to its south is decorated with stones, trees and flowers.

Tuisiyuan Garden (Garden for Retreat and Contemplation) Situated in Wujiang County, 18 kilometers to the west of Suzhou, this garden was built in the period from the 11th to the 13th year of the Guangxu reign of the Qing Dynasty. Occupying an area of more than 6,000 square meters, the garden is divided into two parts, the western part being the residence, the eastern part the garden. The garden again has two sectors, the middle garden and the inner garden. The middle garden was where the master entertained his guests. The buildings there include Zuochun Wangyue Lou (Hall for Enjoying the Moon and Luxuriating in Spring), Suihan Ju (Residence for the Cold Months), and Yingbin Guan (House for Welcoming Guests).The stones, pavilions, flowers and trees in the inner garden are all arranged round the lake in the center. The main building in this quarter was named Tuisi Caotang (Thatched Cottage for Retreat and Contemplation), with Lanjing Ge (Storied Pavilion for Gathering Lovely Scenes) on its left, and Qin Fang (Room for Playing the Zither) on its right, both connected to the main building by a winding roofed walkway. On the west side of the lake is Shuixiang Xie (Fragrant Water Waterside Pavilion), and on its south, a land boat Naohongyige (Big Land Boat), which has a roofed walkway to the rear. On the east side of the lake is a rockery, and lying high up on it, Mianyun Ting (Pavilion Reposing in Clouds). On the southern side of the water are Xintai platform and a small waterside pavilion named Guyushenliang (Cold Rain on Mushrooms). The uniqueness of this garden lies in its compactness, the low scale buildings, and their relation to the water.

Quite a number of distinguished garden architects emerged in the Qing Dynasty, and most of them were from the area to the south of the Yangtze

Scenery in the garden to the southeast as seen from Shuixiang Xie, Tuisiyuan Garden

On the left is the main building of the garden, Tuisi Caotang (Thatched Cottage of Retreat and Contemplation). The terrace in front of the hall is built out onto the water. In the center, there is the high rockery and Mianyun Ting (Pavilion Reposing in Clouds). Guyushengliang (Cold Rain on Mushrooms) stands on the right.

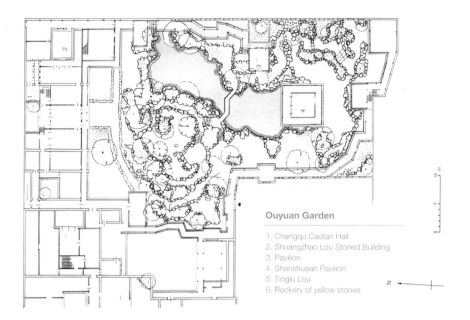

Ouyuan Garden

1. Chengqu Caotan Hall
2. Shuangzhao Lou Storied Building
3. Pavilion
4. Shanshuijian Pavilion
5. Tinglu Lou
6. Rockery of yellow stones

River. Zhang Ran, one of the well-known garden architects who designed imperial gardens, was the son of Zhang Lian, the famous garden architect who lived and worked towards the end of the Ming Dynasty. The most famous was Ge Yuliang, who created many a fine garden and wrote books on garden building. As was recorded, he used stone hooks of different sizes to hold the rocks together, and therefore the rockeries built under his supervision lasted. Li Yu was one of the famous garden architects in the northern part of China. Several gardens in Beijing were built under his supervision.

During the Qing Dynasty, private gardens developed at a faster rate than ever before. The increase in city population and the ensuing shortage of land for gardens meant that the Qing gardens were generally smaller in scale than the Ming ones, and some were developed on the basis of old gardens. Such being the situation, artificial elements began to play a more important role in the garden, and flowers, trees and water surface became less significant. In Ming times, buildings had occupied about 15% of the total area of a garden, whereas in the Qing period, the percentage rose to 30%. More buildings were put up in gardens to meet the higher living standards of their owners. Thus, the art of "creating the limitless within a limited space" became the most important of the

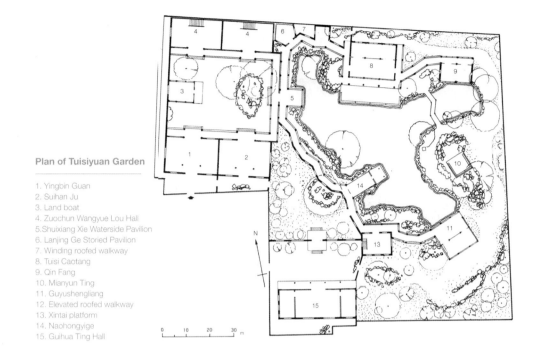

Plan of Tuisiyuan Garden

1. Yingbin Guan
2. Suihan Ju
3. Land boat
4. Zuochun Wangyue Lou Hall
5. Shuixiang Xie Waterside Pavilion
6. Lanjing Ge Storied Pavilion
7. Winding roofed walkway
8. Tuisi Caotang
9. Qin Fang
10. Mianyun Ting
11. Guyushengliang
12. Elevated roofed walkway
13. Xintai platform
14. Naohongyige
15. Guihua Ting Hall

garden art. The use of buildings for spatial division became a common practice, and sometimes, buildings with no practical function were erected purely for this purpose. The layout of private gardens during the Qing Dynasty was in effect a laying-out of buildings of diverse form and function.

Roofed walkways were, to a large extent, built to serve a variety of purposes: they could be used as a perambulatory, to provide shelter from the elements, and to frame or form scenery. Rocks and stones were increasingly used as well. They were generally employed to line the embankment of lakes, or to project onto the water surface. Such ideas were only feasible in a small garden, the expense of lining the embankment of a large lake being so great. The most significant achievement of Qing garden architects was to build rockeries in small gardens to simulate natural cliffs, peaks and deep valleys. Ge Yuliang and Li Yu were true masters of the art. The treatment of water surface also advanced, and islands, pavilions in the center of lakes, zigzag bridges and short dykes were used to divide up the water surface with the aim of creating scenery of greater depth. In general it can be said that the era of the Qing Dynasty led to private gardens being created in a more ornate style than those of the previous periods.

Artistic Characteristics of Private Gardens

—— The beauty of primitive simplicity, The merging of poetry in natural scenery, A walk through a scroll painting

The merging of poetic sentiments and picturesque concepts in gardens and creating gardens no less beautiful than nature itself: these were the underlying principles of the garden art in China.

I. The Outlook on Nature and the Aesthetic Taste of Men of Letters

China's men of letters were strongly influenced by both Confucianism and Taoism, the former philosophy being the highest principle that guided their life and aesthetic standards. However, it was the Taoist philosophy, which expounded a pessimistic and resigned world outlook, that had borne a more direct impact on the development of gardens, which, as has been explained previously, originated from the hermit ideology. Generally speaking, a scholar was a faithful disciple of Confucianism while experiencing success, but would seek consolation in Taoist philosophy when he became disappointed or his

Haopujian, Beihai

This is a quiet garden within a garden located on the eastern shore of the Taiye Lake in Beihai. A bridge connects Linshui Xuan (Waterside Pavilion) with the stone arch at the entrance. The name of the garden Haopujian was taken from the story of Zhuang Zi arguing with his friend about the happiness of the fish. "Hao" was the name of the river where Zhuang Zi stood and watched the fish swimming leisurely about in the water.

career had failed. Confucian philosophy, as reflected in the Book of Changes, advocated the "interplay between Heaven and Man". Confucianists believed that nature was the ultimate aesthetic standard. All that were in accord with nature could effect an interplay between Heaven and Man; and man could be tempered by nature and thus achieve moral perfection. Taoists believed in the perfection of nature, and the "oneness of Heaven and Man". One should seek absolution in the embrace of nature, thereby forgetting success or failure, happiness or sorrow, and henceforth arriving at a complete merging of the self in nature, and achieving the ultimate value of human life. Taoism believed in the return of man to nature.

Both philosophies had a strong influence on the development of the private garden. It was the Taoist admiration for nature which brought about the desire to build gardens to simulate its beauty; and it was the Confucian aesthetic aspirations that gave birth to such standards for garden building as "although man-made, yet no less beautiful than the creations of nature herself".

The story of how the famous Taoist philosopher Zhuang Zi felt the happiness of the fish can serve to illustrate the relationship between Taoist aesthetic principles and gardens. Zhuang Zi, standing on a bridge over the River Hao and watching the fish swimming about in the water, said, "Look how leisurely the fish is swimming in the water. That is an expression of its happiness." Hui Zi said to his friend, "You are not the fish. How do you know it is happy?" Zhuang Zi replied, "You are not I. How do you know that I do

Zhiyu Qiao, Xiequ Yuan

Xiequ Yuan (Garden of Harmonious Interest) is another garden within a garden in the northeast corner of the Summer Palace, and modeled on the Jichangyuan Garden in Wuxi. It is arranged with the lake in the center, surrounded by buildings. The name of the bridge Zhiyu Qiao (Fish Knowing Bridge) also originates from the story of Zhuang Zi and the happiness of fish.

not know the fish is happy?" By watching the fish, he felt its happiness. The happiness of man was realized through the happiness of the fish; man lived in the happiness of the fish. The impact of this story about the "oneness of nature and man" on private gardens was manifested in many ways, one of the most obvious examples being the names given to scenic spots. There was one in Beihai Park in Beijing named Haopujian. "Hao" was the name of the river where Zhuang Zi had observed the happiness of the fish. A bridge in Xiequyuan (Garden of Harmonious Interest) in the Summer Palace in Beijing was given the name of Fish-Knowing Bridge. Both names reflect the Taoist belief in the "oneness of nature and man".

Another traditional Chinese philosophical concept was the "transfer of feelings", which was, in a way, similar to Zhuang Zi's understanding of the fish. According to the Confucian belief in the "interaction of feelings between Heaven and Man", all phenomena in the universe possessed feelings comparable to human sentiments. For example, the great Song Dynasty painter Guo Xi wrote, "In spring when mountains emit vapour-like clouds, one feels happy and joyful. In summer when mountains are shaded by luxuriant trees, one feels confident and calm. In autumn when the air in the mountains is limpid and leaves fall in the passing wind, one feels solemn and depressed. In winter when the mountains are shrouded in a gloomy haze, one feels dreary and forlorn." In the eyes of a painter, "Mountains in spring appear to be smiling; mountains in summer give a joyful impression; mountains in autumn appear to be charmingly attired; mountains in winter seem to be reposing in peace." The belief in the "transfer of feelings" and the "interaction between Heaven and Man" is clearly illustrated by such a text.

Another important aspect of traditional Chinese aesthetics was "the beauty of constant motion". According to the Book of Changes, the universe was in constant motion, and so were art and aesthetics. The beauty of motion was best expressed in Chinese calligraphy, which also had an important role to play in the private garden. The contour of hills, the tortuous roads, and the free curves of the embankments of pools and lakes were also expressions of the beauty of motion. Even the geometric form of a building could be softened by the curves of the dramatically upturned eaves of the roofs. All the lines, curves and contours in a garden were woven together to achieve a balance of motion, just as what was expressed in calligraphy.

For men of letters, the sole criterion for judging aesthetic value was the

A view of the garden to the north from Hanbi Shanfang, Liuyuan Garden

The two gigantic ginko trees and the small pavilion form an interesting contrast. The zigzag bridge and the isle, and their reflection in the water, are a fascinating sight.

word "refined", which meant "high taste" in general. For example, a piece of art should be simple in form, of graceful line, subdued in colour, and harmonious in a general way. This aesthetic standard was applied to all aspects of life, including clothing, articles for daily use, the style of furniture, the binding of books, stationery articles, tea cups, as well as houses and gardens. For a scholar, a house did not have to be showy, nor the flowers and trees in bright colours. A few bamboos and stones if well arranged could lend a house a refinement that would emit the "fragrance of books".

Colour was another important factor. Gold, scarlet and bright green were colours used in imperial palaces and gardens, but were considered unacceptable for gardens of the literati. Like the ink-and-wash landscape paintings, the colour scheme in such gardens was generally a combination of black, white, grey and maroon.

Anything "old" was considered refined: this was another aesthetic factor extensively applied in gardens of the literati. By "old" it meant articles that had been tempered by time, and so were more pleasant to the eye than new ones. For example, bronze ware spotted with greenish verdigris, moss-covered stones, stone steps with edges and corners eroded by time, ornaments and paints whose colour had faded showed a maturation through time, and therefore had a more refined and tasteful air.

II. Literature and Gardens

Writing essays and composing poems were the most important accomplishment that, for men of letters, could lead to a higher social standing, and they had both direct or indirect impact on garden building.

It was considered that a good essay, one which aroused the interest of readers, should be composed of four parts: the prelude, the development of the theme, an argument from different angles, and the conclusion. This method of essay writing was eventually applied to the garden art, the most successful example being Liuyuan Garden (Lingering Garden) in Suzhou.

As in an essay, the garden begins with a remarkable prelude. Upon entering the main gate, one first comes to a corridor about 50 meters in length and lined on both sides with high walls. Led by the corridor to the right and then to the left, the visitor passes through several small verandas or yards, some dark and some bright, before finally arriving at the waterside pavilion Gumujiaoke (Interwined Old Trees). Here at last one would expect to have a full view of the garden, but due to a row of open-tracery windows on the north side of Gumujiaoke, one can have no more but a glimpse of the garden behind. The route now continues westward, leading to a small pavilion Luyin (Green Shade). There the whole garden, with its rockeries and lake, suddenly opens out before one, so glorious that in spite of having been slowly prepared, one is nevertheless overwhelmed. This was the "development" of the leitmotif in essay writing. One can now sojourn in the main hall Hanbi Shanfang (Cold Emerald Green Mountain Lounge) and enjoy the scenery. The lake, the isle, the rockeries, the pavilions, bridges, and roofed walkways all lie before one, so perfect that one could have the feeling of being completely immersed in a poem or having entered a scroll landscape painting. By going upstairs in the Mingse Lou (Bright Zither Storied Building), one is treated to an overall view of the garden. To the northwest of the main hall, there are two routes, one up the hill and the other along the waterside, each allowing visitors to enjoy the scenery from different angles. This is the "argument" stage in an essay. The route through the hill leads to Wenmuxuxiang Xuan (Veranda for Smelling the Fragrance of Sweet-Scented Osmanthus), from where one has a view of the scenery in the east. The winding

Open-tracery windows, Liuyuan Garden

Liuyuan Garden is famous for its open-tracery windows, through which the scenery in the garden can only be glimpsed. The diversity of tracery is remarkable.

roofed walkway takes one to the back of the hill where trees and bamboos grow in profusion, and at the end of the walkway stands Yuancui Ge (Pavilion of Distant Green). Looking into the southwesterly direction, one can see hills in the distance and water in the foreground. The other route is along the waterside, which also begins at the main hall. It leads to the pavilion Ke Ting standing in the centre of the north hill, and from here one has a full view of the southern part of the lake. A path from the pavilion leads down to the waterside, and by crossing the bridge one reaches Little Penglai Island and further on Haoputing Pavilion. From here, one has a view across the lake, Gumujiaoke, Luyin and Mingse Lou, reminding one of the scenery first seen on entering the garden. There, the beginning and the end of the tour meet, and that is the "conclusion" part of an essay.

Gardens were enriched by the use of such poetic elements as sentiments and associations. The Tang poet Wang Wei was the first to begin this tradition of describing the beauty of a garden in poems. His poem Dwelling amidst Bamboos quoted previously presented to the reader a picture of a lonely hermit playing his lute in bamboo groves by the light of the moon. The scenery in a garden was thus brought to a much higher realm of perfect harmony between man and nature.

Poetry in gardens usually took the form of couplets or tablets. The couplets were generally hung on the two sides of an entrance; they could be newly composed or quotations of lines from famous poems. Names given to buildings in gardens were always written in handsome calligraphy, carved on tablets and hung in the center of the beam. They reflected the literary accomplishments of the owner of the garden. The names given could be descriptions of the scenery surrounding the building, or they could be taken from some story to arouse associations. For example, the name Whom-to-Sit-with Pavilion in the Zhuozhengyuan Garden in Suzhou was taken from a poem by the famous Song poet Su Dongpo: "Whom do I sit with? The moon, gentle breezes, and myself."

The hanging of couplets on buildings was one of the important features in gardens. They enabled the owner of the garden to express his ideas and sentiments, his aim in building the garden, a description of the scenery, philosophical meditations, or reminiscences of the past. The couplets were generally written by famous calligraphers. While enjoying the couplets as valuable

Shanshuijian, Ouyuan Garden

Shanshuijian (Amid Mountains and Water), a waterside pavilion located at the southern end of the lake, is an ideal place for enjoying the surrounding scenery, and conveys the impression of being surrounded by mountains and water.

Liuting Ge, Zhuozhengyuan Garden

Located on the western shore of the lake in the western section of the garden, Liuting Ge (Stay-and-Listen Pavilion) is a bright and spacious building with full-length windows on four sides. Two rare examples of full-length openwork screens can be seen inside, one of ginko wood carved with patterns of pine, bamboo, plum blossoms and birds, the other of Nanmu wood carved with patterns of dragons. The rain pattering on the broad lotus leaves in autumn has a poetic quality.

pieces of literature, one could also enjoy the art of calligraphy. They were part of the garden architecture, meant not only for decoration, but for enhancing the cultural ambiance of the garden as well.

III. Painting and Gardens

Gardens in a sense had their origin in landscape painting. For a very long period in ancient China, there were no professional garden builders. The owners of gardens were either painters themselves, or invited famous painters to do the planning and design for them. Wang Wei of Tang, Emperor Huizong of Song, Ni Zan of Yuan, Wen Zhenming of Ming, and Shi Tao and Li Yu of Qing were all great painters, and experts in garden building as well. It was not until the late

Ming Dynasty that professional garden architects such as Zhang Lian and Ji Cheng began to emerge. Ji Cheng, according to his book On Garden Building, learned to paint when he was young, and was a great admirer of the painters in ancient times. He designed gardens in the same way as an artist painted: they both turned the scenery close to their hearts into reality. In his comments on Ji Cheng's On Garden Building, Kan Duo wrote, "Mountain building actually derives from landscape painting. Painters call hills and vales into being with their paint brush and ink, whereas garden builders create them using rocks and earth. Although different in substance, the guiding principle is the same."

Painting, for men of letters, was not only the most important of the arts but also the most refined. It was through painting that man was able to bring into realization the beauty of nature in all its forms. Landscape painting had its origin in nature, but was more condensed and concentrated. In garden building, therefore, the ultimate aim was to endow the garden with the sublime concepts expressed in paintings. All the scenes presented to the viewer, regardless of whether he was moving along or sitting still, staying indoors or walking along a path, should be like a framed picture. He should be made to feel as if he were strolling through a scroll painting.

Painters built gardens as artists. The arrangement of the scenic spots, the sites for building hills and lakes, for planting trees and flowers, and for putting

up various types of buildings, required the same comprehensive planning as a landscape painting. Design followed the theories of painting, since there was little theory on the art of garden building in those days. The great Tang painter Wang Wei wrote in his Artifice on Mountain-and-Water Painting: "The first step is to determine the major and minor roles of all the phenomena in a drawing. The second step is to decide what is to be in the foreground and what in the background. Then comes the decision on all the elements that will make up the scenery, and whether they should be placed high or low in the picture." Jing Hao of the Five Dynasties era (907-960) wrote in his Main Points on Mountain-and-Water Painting: "Regarding mountain peaks, there should be major and minor ones. As for water, it should have its source and destination. Mountains should be intricate, and peaks and cliffs should look majestic. Roads should be forked, streams should appear indistinctly in some parts, and river banks should rise and fall in an undulating manner." Da Chongguang wrote in his On Painting: "---- Mountains are static, but if the water is made to flow, the whole picture will be in motion. Stones are still, but if the trees are made to live, the painting will be endowed with a living spirit." These theories on painting, and many more could be cited, all served as the guiding principles for the art of garden building. They were especially valuable when it came to the building of artificial hills, for the success of a garden largely depended on the artistry of its hills and rockeries.

Layout Plan and Design

—— To create the limitless within a limited space, To integrate the solemn and subdued with the charming and bright

The artistic and cultural value of the private gardens lay in their perfect spatial coordination. The gardens thus created could stand the most critical scrutiny and would draw viewers on by means of an endless series of attractive sights. What made these gardens such a unique achievement was the "dynamic beauty" of the landscape.

I. Garden and Residence

Private gardens were always attached to the residence, and commonly located to the rear or by the side of the mansion. In feudal society, the residential quarters for the female members of the family were always located in the innermost courtyards of the residence, and so it was more convenient for the ladies of the house to have the garden at the back. Private gardens in those days were not open to the public, the only exception being Shuiyuan Garden in Nanjing, which was not enclosed within a wall. Liuyuan Garden in Suzhou was provided with a special entrance for guests.

Kansongduhua Xuan, Wangshiyuan Garden

Hall hidden behind rocks and trees, Kansongduhua Xuan (Veranda for Enjoying Pine Trees and Deriving Joy from Paintings) used to be the studio of the former owner of the garden. It is the main building on the north side of the lake.

When it came to the Qing Dynasty, and a rise in living standards, gardens had to meet the growing material requirements of their owners. As a result, more buildings were put up in gardens to serve not only as residences, but as studies, studios or halls for entertaining guests. In large private gardens, there was generally a clear division between the different functions.

II. The Layout of Hills, Rockeries and Water

Hills and water played the most important part in a garden, and their scale and shape were determined by the size of the garden and the topography of the land. There were basically three types of layout: a layout with water as the leitmotif; an arrangement with hills as the theme; or a balanced arrangement of hills and water. There was hardly a garden without water, and most private gardens in the area to the south of the Yangtze River had water as their leitmotif. Not many gardens had hills as their main feature because the building of artificial hills required great artistry and high cost. The third type of layout was mostly adopted for gardens of larger scale.

Water as the leitmotif To have the lake at the center with buildings and scenic spots encircling it was a layout that was considered to achieve the best result. Water was an enlivening element, reflecting the blue sky, white clouds and the surrounding scenery and so achieving spatial depth. Plants, such as lotus flowers, could be grown in the water, and bridges and dykes built over it to give pleasure.

The layout of the area of water could be planned in a number of ways. In

Zhuwaiyizhi Xuan, Wangshiyuan Garden

Located in the northeastern corner of the lake, Zhuwaiyizhi Xuan (Veranda of the Slanting Bamboo Twig) is connected with the Sheya Lang (Duck-shooting Roofed Walkway) on the east side of the lake. From there one can see the scenery round the lake.

a small garden, there was generally only one lake, whereas in a large one, there could be one central lake, connected with several minor stretches of water, which could take the form of a waterfall, a stream or a brook. Lakes were always given irregular shapes to simulate natural stretches of water, but in certain specific circumstances, the embankments were made straight or zigzaged to set off the buildings in the vicinity.

This type of layout was mostly adopted when the land was flat and there was not much variation in elevation. The plans of Wangshiyuan Garden and Tuisiyuan Garden are typical examples. In the former, the main building Kansongduhua Xuan (Veranda for Enjoying Pine Trees and Deriving Joy from Paintings) to the north of the lake, and Jixu Zhai (Study of the Ethereal), and Zhuwaiyizhi Xuan (Veranda of the Slanting Bamboo Twig) to its east are comparatively large and occupy a commanding position in the garden. From these buildings, an overall view of the scenery round the lake can be had. Between the east bank of the lake and the west wall of the residential mansion, there is only a narrow strip of land decorated with a few stones, trees and flowers, and with the whitewashed wall as a background, it possesses an intimate charm all of its own. On the west side of the lake, there is a curved roofed walkway intersected by a small pavilion protruding onto the water, a treatment that adds interest to the otherwise straight boundary wall. To the south of the lake is Zuoyin Shuige (Tassel-Washing Waterside Pavilion), half of which lying over the water, and a yellow stone rockery. The lake and the area round it form the centrepiece of the garden, and although the buildings and landscape elements all differ in shape and style, dimension and spacing are perfect. This is one of the most tranquil and beautiful garden scenes in China. The layout of the Tuisiyuan Garden is also centered round an irregularly shaped lake, and the most imposing site is the rockery of Taihu stones lying on its eastern bank, with a pavilion on its top. Halls, pavilions, towers, land boats and terraces are situated round the rest of the lake, all of different dimension and shape, but again appropriately spaced and connected by a winding roofed walkway.

Rockeries as the leitmotif Gardens of this type might lack the charm and liveliness of the type mentioned above, but can convey the splendour and vastness of a mountainous region, and its attraction for one wishing to lead the life of a recluse. Grand rockeries are not mere static objects, but take visitors upwards to the top, into its mysterious grottos, or through its valley-like openings. The principal building in the garden usually faces the front of the rockery so that the most attractive side is seen first, but the others are also important in that they allow the scenic delights to be enjoyed from a vantage point.

Water is also an indispensable element in this type of garden as it enhances the splendor of the rockeries, acting as a foil. The most outstanding examples of this type are Ouyuan Garden (Twin Garden), Canglangting (Surging-Wave Pavilion Garden), Huanxiushanzhuang (Mountain Villa with Beautiful Surrounding Scenery) in Suzhou, Yuyuan Garden (Happy Garden) in Shanghai, and Geyuan Garden in Yangzhou. The grand yellow stone rockery in Ouyuan Garden is particularly magnificent, with its splendid and commanding east section, the small and low west section, and the valley between them, one meter wide. The lower part of the rockery comprises huge rocks, and trees grow in profusion on the upper part. The east side of the hill takes the form of a precipice with a lake lying at its foot. The view of the rockery from the main building of the garden to the north resembles a landscape painting by the great Yuan master Huang Gongwang.

Balanced arrangement of rockeries and water Most of the private gardens in existence today are of this type, including Zhuozhengyuan Garden, Liuyuan Garden, Yiyuan Garden, Shizilin Garden in Suzhou, Jichangyuan Garden in Wuxi, Qiuxia Pu (Orchard in Autumn Evening Glow) in Shanghai, and Qiyuan Garden (Charming Garden) in Zhejiang Province. In the layout of these gardens, neither the hills nor the water surface dominates as far as the spatial design is concerned. Their integration was planned in a variety of ways, creating gardens that are full of life and breathtakingly beautiful.

In this kind of arrangement, rockeries and lakes were arranged in such a way that whatever angle the different scenery was viewed from, one would have the impression that one was looking at a landscape painting. If one took a walk in the garden, endless surprises would be waiting at every turn of the path. The most typical example is Zhuozengyuan Garden in Suzhou, where the main building Yuanxiang Tang (Hall of Distant Fragrance) is in the south while the rockeries and lake are located in the north. The view of these south-facing rockeries and the lake is forever changing as the day, with its different moods, passes, and the observer moves on to a new vantage point. What one sees before him is a scroll painting gradually being unrolled. Two small pavilions stand on the top of the two high rockeries to the north with a stream flowing between them. A low zigzag bridge crosses the spacious lake that surrounds the rockeries on all sides. The southern end of the lake has a long spur, crossed by the Little

Flying Rainbow bridge. Such treatment not only gave the water surface depth but made the lake appear endless. In Liuyuan Garden, the rockeries are located in the northwest, and the lake in the southeast, with a small channel built into the rockeries to suggest the fountain head of the water.

III. Spatial Organization

The aim of spatial organization was to create the impression of the limitless in a highly limited space, and give the garden intricacy. In ancient times, people did not have a scientific spatial concept, yet, when gardens were built in the way that paintings were drawn or essays written, the result could be spectacular.

Generally speaking, private gardens were made up of a series of spatial units, each with its own function and distinguishing characteristics. Large gardens might be divided into several primary or subsidiary spatial units, whereas small gardens might only have one spatial unit. The division of space was effected by means of stones, trees and flowers, buildings, or walls. Consequently, there were basically two types of spatial techniques: one using natural materials (such as stones, rocks and plants), the other man-made substances (such as buildings and walls). The former could bring about a free and natural atmosphere, whereas the

Yellow stone artificial hill, Ouyuan Garden

Ouyuan Garden has hills as its theme. The yellow stone hill there is so intricately built that a walk up it is like a real mountain ramble. It is one of the most outstanding artificial hills in the gardens of Suzhou.

Xiaofeihong, Zhuozhengyuan Garden / opposite page

Spanning the water next to Xiangzhou (Fragrant Isle), Xiaofeihong (Little Flying Rainbow) is the only corridor bridge in the gardens of Suzhou. Looking north from Xiaocanglang pavilion, one can see Hefengsimian Ting (Pavilion with Lotus and Breezes on Four Sides) and Jianshan Lou (Storied Building with a View of Mountains) beyond the corridor bridge.

latter could suggest an artificial but aesthetic ambiance. In addition to these two types, spaces could also be divided by a mixture of both natural and man-made elements, including buildings, rockeries and plants.

As to the spatial layout of a unit, it could either be open or enclosed, or partly open and partly enclosed as an alternative. An open spatial unit always created a bright and cheerful atmosphere, whereas an enclosed unit usually conveyed a quiet and lonely feeling.

A spatial unit could be formal and rigid, with clearly defined functional characteristics. Another type of spatial unit might be free and functionally ambiguous, the latter type forming the basis for the private garden.

Spatial units could also be of different size; they could be light or shady, direct or intricate. The art of spatial organization lay in the garden builder's ability to integrate spatial units of different type and form, and achieve diversity, contrast and harmony.

In a garden, there should be spatial division on the one hand, and spatial linkage on the other to provide a variety of views that would delight and enable one to stroll from one part of the garden to another. One could pass from enclosed spatial units to open ones, from formal spatial units enclosed mainly by buildings to natural ones, from small units to large units, and from units with clearly defined characteristics to those with ambiguous features. Such was spatial linkage, and the ever-changing nature of the spatial units would attract the visitor and arouse his curiosity and interest. For example, the 50-meter long corridor leading from the entrance gate to the main spatial unit in Liuyuan Garden is a stimulating experience and not merely a transitory passage, and can be compared to the overture or prelude of a symphony. It was designed to consist of a series of spaces, large or small, bright or dark, that would draw people on. Visitors would be led to turn right and left until the climax was reached, the bright and open spatial unit with the lake and rockeries. The change is so unexpected that it is almost dramatic.

The visual linkage between spatial units enables the visitor to see another or even a third spatial unit from where he is standing. He is thus given the illusion that the garden is much larger and deeper than it actually is. The technique involved was to arrange a variety of door and window openings between two spatial units. These could take the form of perforated or flowery windows, possibly decorated with tracery or latticework, moon- or vase-shaped door openings, perhaps decorated with couplets, and tablets. Through these openings, one would be able to see some of the spatial units on the other side. One would not, however, be able, nor was one encouraged, to have a full view of the scenery beyond; only a glimpse was allowed. In some cases, it was through the light reflected through the door or window openings that one could sense the existence of another spatial unit beyond, and then one would let imagination take over, and associations would flood the mind. This particular spatial treatment in private gardens was sometimes referred to as the "art of concealment".

IV. The Borrowing of Scenery

This was one of the important techniques used in the planning and design of Chinese gardens. Beautiful scenery could be "borrowed" from outside, or scenery in the garden itself could be so designed that one scenic spot could

Hill-ascending roofed walkway, Canglangting Garden

The walkway runs along the east boundary wall of the garden. In the middle section, there is a semi-pavilion containing a stele. The rather monotonous whitewashed wall is lent interest by the decorative windows with their diverse traceries.

serve as a "borrowed view" for the other. According to On Garden Building, "The borrowing of scenery is one of the most important artistic techniques in garden building. Views can be borrowed from afar, from nearby, from up above, from down below, or from the changing of seasons." This omni-directional and dynamic "borrowing" of views gave the scenery in a garden such richness and vivacity that a visitor could hardly attend to all the beautiful sights at once.

Not every garden had views to be borrowed from outside. If there was such an opportunity, a line of sight to the object would be carefully planned so that the view was drawn into the garden. A classical example was the "borrowing" of the view of the pagoda on top of Xishan Hill and incorporating it into the Jichangyuan Garden in Wuxi. Standing at the northern end of the slender-shaped lake and looking south, one can see the inverted reflection of the Xishan pagoda in the water; one can hardly tell whether the scene is in or out of the garden.

The aim of borrowing views from outside was to introduce artistic concepts into the garden art, to extend the space beyond its limits, and to enrich the scenery. It was not only scenery that could be "borrowed"; forms, sounds,

Crabapple flower-shaped door opening, Shizilin Garden

This door opening leads to the courtyard to the north of the small square hall, and provides an interesting "frame" for the scenery.

colours and fragrances were also incorporated into gardens.

The borrowing of forms Techniques such as "creating scenic focal points", "framing scenery" or "permeating scenery" were often adopted to create, either in the foreground or in the distance, set-pieces for the delight of the onlooker, using the architecture, garden furniture, rockeries, stones and plants.

The borrowing of sounds This technique, if handled appropriately and innovatively, could add greatly to the scenery in a garden. The beautiful world of sound could be incorporated into the garden, and thus arouse endless associations. The chime of bells in distant temples at dawn or at dusk, the sound of water flowing in brooks in mountain valleys, the pattering of rain on the broad leaves of banana trees on autumn evenings, and the singing of birds in willows on warm spring days could all be "borrowed" to create a poetic atmosphere in an architectural environment.

The borrowing of colours Moonlight, if it can be seen as a kind of colour, was often "borrowed" to enhance the beauty of a scenic spot. There were many classical examples, such as Santanyingyue (Three Pools Mirroring the Moon) and Pinghuqiuyue (Autumn Moon over a Calm Lake) in Hangzhou, Zhejiang Province, Yueshe Jiangsheng Island (Island of Moonlight and Sound of River) and Lihua Banyue Courtyard (Courtyard of Pear Blossoms Accompanying the

Moon), two scenic spots in the Summer Resort at Chengde. The charm of these famous scenic spots is closely related to the "colour" of the moon.

The ever-changing hue of clouds, the tender green weeping willows and pink peach blossoms that heralded in spring, the red wintersweets that welcomed the snow, and the crimson maple leaves adorning autumn hills could all be taken into consideration when drawing up plans for view-borrowing.

The borrowing of fragrances The fragrance of plants could add to the charm of gardens, and so could also be "borrowed", or taken into consideration when designing a garden. Lanpu Garden in Guangzhou was famous for its orchids, and their fragrance made the garden a famous attraction. The lotus flower was a favorite plant in classical gardens, not only for its shape, but for its fragrance as well. Hefengsimian Ting (Pavilion with Lotus and Breezes on Four Sides) in Zhuozhengyuan Garden is a typical example of how a scenic spot was planned by "borrowing" the fragrance of lotus flowers.

The technique of spatial organization was closely related to the artistry of view-borrowing, and whether a garden builder succeeded in establishing this relationship depended on his cultural accomplishment. In garden design, importance was always attached to the harmonious coordination of the artificial and the natural, of the buildings and the landscape. When there was no appropriate scenic object to be "borrowed", objects such as garden furniture, rocks and stones, or flowers and trees could be specifically planned as views to be "borrowed" and incorporated into certain spatial units. This technique was prevalent in ancient classical gardens, and can be found in gardens built in recent years as well.

The building of rockeries and the handling of water were the two most important aspects of garden construction, and the former was an especially specific technique in ancient times. Since private gardens in cities were practically all laid out on flat land, the most important task was to dig lakes and build rockeries.

The Building of Hills and Rockeries and the Handling of Water

—— Harmonious integration of the splendour of mountains with lakes, pools and brooks in deep valleys

I. The Building of Hills and Rockeries

Artificial hills in gardens could be built of earth, stones or a mixture of the two. However, as hills piled up entirely with earth inevitably occupied a large area, and their height was limited, this kind of hill was hardly ever built in small private gardens. Hills built with a mixture of earth and stones were therefore usual. Rockeries were often built in small courtyards for decoration. Individual stones of unique or peculiar shapes could be placed at certain spots to enhance the scenery.

Rockeries built with a mixture of earth and stones had several advantages. They were labour and material saving, and it was easy to give them the required shape. The rockery was piled up layer after layer, with earth inside and stones outside. The stones helped stabilize the earth, while the earth was indispensable for growing plants. Trees grew in the course of time, their roots going deep down into the earth. Earth and stones gradually became one, and in time the rockery looked no less beautiful than a natural hill.

A grand rockery needed space, and the aim was to create a work of art just as intricate and varied as a landscape painting. The layout and design of such a rockery largely depended on the cultural skills of the designer.

A hill was made up of three parts: the foot, the middle part, and the ridge. Ideally it had to have varying shapes and contours, the features of mountains, their peaks and precipices, valleys, caverns and streams all serving as models for the rockery. Generally, the first step was to determine the location and size of the main peak, and then the subsidiary and minor peaks.

Grand rockery hill, Yuyuan Garden

Rising up to 12 meters, the yellow stone rockery boasts a formidable precipice, a deep valley, a flowing stream, and a profusion of trees. A masterpiece of the famous Ming Dynasty garden builder Zhang Nanyang, the rockery represents a rare example of the art of rockery building to be found in private gardens.

The process of rockery making began with a close scrutiny of each piece of stone collected for use. For the ancient masters, this procedure of "studying stones" was an especially important and indispensable procedure, each stone being appraised before finally being chosen. For a rockery, only one single kind of stone was acceptable; a combination of two or more kinds was never allowed. The stones collected for use all differed in shape, grain, and colour. They could have the shape of slabs, plates, piers, arches or wedges, and have a straight or slanting grain. The colour of a stone depended, to a large extent, on its natural state. A stone that had been lying in the sun would look quite different in texture than one that had been in the shade, and the moss on the surface would also be different. The art was to group stones of similar texture and colour together to simulate the natural conditions in which they were found.

Another important aspect of rockery-making was the technique of piecing the stones together and treating their convex and concave sides. The juxtaposition of stones according to grain and texture gave the rockery the appearance of a miniature mountain, with its folds, ledges and crevices. The process was seen as restoring the stones to their natural habitat --- a transcendence of the artificial, the essence of China's gardens.

Just as in the construction of a house, a rockery needed a strong foundation because stones were heavy and plain earth could hardly sustain the load. Before piling up the stones, a foundation of wood or lime was first laid, going down to

Taihu stones, Yiyuan Garden

These curious-lookig stones stand in the courtyard between the Baishi Xuan (Veranda in Honour of Stones) and Poxian Qinguan (Celestial Zither House). Stones were honoured by men of letters for their associative power.

Stone path up the high rockery, Ouyuan Garden / opposite page

Large yellow stones stand vertically at the "entrance" to the rockery. The size of the stones becomes smaller as the path climbs the hill. The purpose of such careful arrangement is to give an impression of the rockery's spatial depth. The laying out of stones of varying sizes, shapes and grains to form a harmonious whole displays great artistry.

a depth of about 1 meter below ground level. The body of the rockery above the foundation was the most complicated and intricate section because this was where the grottos, valleys, cliffs and precipices would be built. Garden builders in ancient times accumulated a wealth of experience and developed a series of techniques of binding the stones together to guarantee structural safety.

The treatment of the topmost section of the rockery gave it its contour and skyline, and was thus an important link in the entire process. It was then that the main peak and subsidiary peaks were shaped. The main peak could be given the form of a standing sword or ax, or be made to look like floating clouds. Subsidiary peaks were smaller in size, and were built to set off the main peak and add to the grandeur and depth of the rockery.

The most complicated task was the building of grottos, which added interest and intricacy to the rockery. Moreover, a large number of stones could thus be conserved. In ancient times, stone strips were used as beams for the grottos. When it came to the Qing Dynasty, the famous garden builder Ge Yuliang applied the principle of the arch to cave building. With this method, he could build large rockeries using a comparatively small number of stones. The rockery

in Huanxiu Shanzhuang (Mountain Villa in Beautiful Surroundings) in Suzhou is
an example of Ge Yuliang's work. In some cases, water was conducted into the
caves to make them more fascinating. The Summer Mountain in Geyuan Garden
in Yangzhou is a case in point.

There were several kinds of rockeries built entirely of stones. They
were referred to as "storied hill", "wall hill", "lake hill" and "courtyard hill"
respectively. "Storied hill" meant a rockery with a pavilion or veranda on top,
in which case the rockery actually served as a stairway. "Wall hill" was a rockery
built against a wall, "lake hill" a rockery built over a lake, and "courtyard hill" a
rockery built in a courtyard which generally had plants accompanying it.

Instead of rockeries, individual stones could be placed in gardens as a
highlight. There were two ways of proceeding: isolated placement and scattered
placement. The former was often applied to large pieces of interestingly shaped
stones. A large stone of bizarre shape could serve as an object all on its own,
like a sculpture. It could be placed at an important spot in the garden as a scenic
focal point. Stones thus treated were mostly Taihu stones, especially favoured by
men of letters. Stones which were tall and slender, perforated and full of cavities

were regarded as the most beautiful and suitable for such purposes. Scattered placement referred to the placing of several rocks together to add interest. They could be placed in an area of transition between artificial and natural spatial units. They could also be placed at intervals at the side of a path or by a bridge in a seemingly random way.

II. The Handling of Water

Water in a garden was the artistic simulation of natural lakes, brooks, streams, springs and waterfalls. The best way of creating water scenery in gardens was to make full use of favourable natural topographic conditions and sources of water. Some early private gardens had illustrated just how fascinating water in a

Pavilion in the center of the lake, Shizilin Garden

Standing in the center of the lake, the pavilion is connected to the land on both sides by a bridge, effectively dividing up the water surface. An artificial waterfall used to cascade down the hill to the west is a novel way of handling water in gardens.

Hebutan, Jichangyuan Garden

Hebutan (Beach where Cranes Walk) is an artificial beach projecting into the water on the west side of the lake, and offering a view of Zhiyujian (Fish Knowing Balustrade) on the other side. The creation of artificial beaches was another way of treating the water surface to make it appear deeper and more extensive.

garden could be. One of the famous examples was the Lushan Thatched Cottage belonging to the famous Tang poet Bai Juyi. To the east of his thatched cottage was a waterfall, which, in the dim light of early morning or evening, resembled a piece of white brocade hanging down from heaven. At night, the waterfall recalled the melodious sound of the zither, or the tinkling of jade ornaments on a woman's dress. To the west of his country house, spring water was conducted down the mountain slope by bamboos split into halves. Drops of water fell like dew drops or strings of pearls on his eaves. In ancient times men of letters and hermits had been fascinated by the effect water could have in a garden, and waterfalls were often the theme of mountain-and-water paintings, or models for gardens. Yet it was hardly possible to have flowing water in private gardens in cities.

Since private gardens were mostly limited in space, water scenery mainly

Huafangzhai, Yiyuan Garden

Huafangzhai (Painted Boat Studio) is a land boat in the western section of the garden. The head of the "boat" protrudes into the water. Although the lake is small, one has the impression that the "boat" is lying in dock. The pavilion on the opposite side of the water and the painted boat studio set off one another.

Yuedaofenglai Ting, Wangshiyuan Garden

The Yuedaofenglai Ting (Pavilion Welcoming the Advent of the Moon and Breezes) stands by the roofed walkway running along the western bank of the lake. Its roof rises high above that of the walkway, thus bringing about a contrast in the skyline.

took the form of lakes or pools. According to On Garden Building, the lake in a garden should occupy about one third of the total area. In a large garden, there might be one big lake, and several minor ones, connected with each other to form a water system. A case in point is Zhuozhengyuan in Suzhou. In small gardens, such as Wangshiyuan Garden, there is only one lake, but this has spurs at the ends to suggest the source of the water. The lake, whether large or small, would generally be subdivided by means of bridges, islands, peninsulas or stepping stones, to make the water surface appear larger than it actually was.

Lakes were always given an irregular shape, although they could be basically square, circular or slender-shaped. Taihu stones, yellow stones or bluish-grey stones were mostly used to line the embankment in a seemingly casual manner to contrast with the exquisitely designed buildings and the compact layout. Practically no earth embankment was ever used in private gardens in the area to the south of the Yangtze River. The erection of waterside buildings round the lake was another important aspect in the creation of water scenery in a garden.

Miniature streams and brooks, generally connected with the lake, could arouse associations in the viewer. One of the examples was the 20-meter long rivulet in the famous Jichangyuan Garden in Wuxi. Being two meters above

Scenery in the central section of Geyuan Garden

To the north of Yiyu Xuan (Hall for Pleasant Rain) there is a pool with Taihu stones as a decorative feature round it. Qingyi Ting (Clear Ripple Pavilion), Hutianzichun (Sprig in a Teapot of Universe) are some of the buildings located nearby.

Flowery wall across the water, Yuyuan Garden

Extending across the water, the whitewashed wall forms a strong contrast to the surrounding trees, flowers and stones. Water runs through the "moon-shaped opening", which is actually formed by the arch of the wall and is inverted reflection in the water.

ground level, the water flowing down into the brook made the sound of a waterfall. The secret behind such treatment lay in the height of the rivulet. It had to be above the viewer's line of sight so as to create the illusion of a brook flowing from a deep mountainous source.

Besides stone-lined embankments, artificial beaches were sometimes an alternative. It was recorded that in the great Tang poet Wang Wei's Wangchuan Resort there was a scenic spot named White Stone Beach. This technique has often been used in gardens built in recent years.

Another way of introducing the element of water into courtyards was the use of huge earthernware vessels. Filled with water, they could be used to breed goldfish, or to plant lotus flowers. In the courtyard of Hanshanshi Temple in Suzhou, vats planted with lotus flowers were placed on both sides of the steps leading into the temple hall. They added a lively element to the otherwise solemn and devotional atmosphere of the courtyard.

The success of water scenery in a garden depended not only on the water surface, but on the handling of the embankment as well. If the bank surrounding a lake was intelligently designed, it would make the water surface look more extensive. Islands, peninsulas, dykes, and rocks projecting into the water were some of the ways often adopted to suit the configuration of the water surface. Whatever the method used, the guiding principle was always to take nature as the one and only model.

Building Forms, Types and Materials
—— Exquisitely refined pavilions, studios, waterside
pavilions and land boats

Buildings in private gardens show such diversity of form and type that they play an important role in China's architectural heritage. Compared with traditional buildings elsewhere, buildings in gardens were not so strictly confined to traditional regulations, and therefore demonstrate much more flexibility in form and style, harmonizing with the overall ambiance.

Generally speaking, no two buildings in a garden should be the same, as diversity of form could give it a lively character. The architectural forms of buildings in gardens in the southern areas were usually light and open to suit the warm climate. The division of internal spatial units and the installation of doors and windows were left to the designer's discretion, and an alternate use of open and enclosed spatial units was one of the approaches often adopted. The eaves were of exquisite craftsmanship, but nevertheless simple and refined. Black, white, grey and maroon were the colours mostly used for buildings in gardens. Against a background of green vegetation, they looked particularly elegant.

Much attention was paid to the design of the roofs in private gardens. The corners of the eaves were turned up so high that, together with the tall trees, they formed a beautiful skyline. The roofs, including the gabled, pyramidal and round-ridge types, were similar to those of other types of buildings, but

Courtyard to the north of Wufeng Xianguan, Liuyuan Garden

Wufeng Xiangguan (Five-Peak Celestial Hall) is the most important hall within the group located in the area. The courtyard is decorated with natural stones and planted with an abundance of trees and flowers.

Roof of Mingse Lou, Liuyuan Garden

Ancient trees and dramatically upturned eaves of roofs very often make for a fascinating skyline in private gardens. The roof of Mingse Lou (Bright Zither Storied Building) is in the round ridge hip-and-gable style, and its double eaves curve up so high up that they look birds soaring into the sky.

Ningxia Ge in Qiuxiapu Garden

Ningxia Ge (Storied Pavilion of Condensed Colourful Clouds) stands in the northernmost courtyard of the garden. It is two storied, and its style is typical of the region to the south of the Yangtze River. The second story of the pavilion offers a splendid view of the garden.

they had more variations to suit the specific features of the environment. For example, the east side of a roof could be in the hip-and-gable style, whereas the west side could be of the gabled sort. This flexibility contributed to the light and cheerful atmosphere in a garden.

There were two types of building, one being functional and the other ornamental. The former included halls for entertaining guests and for family gatherings, and buildings used as studies or studios, whereas the latter included such buildings as pavilions, roofed walkways and land boats. However, these buildings did serve a double function: they satisfied the needs of their owners while being an indispensable part of the scenery in the garden as well.

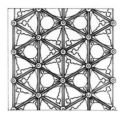

hexagonal six-fragment
linghua pattern

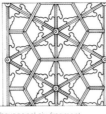

hexagonal six-fragment
linghua pattern

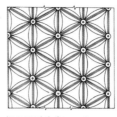

hexagonal six-fragment
linghua pattern

tetragonal four-fragment
linghua pattern

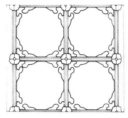

tetragonal four-fragment
linghua pattern

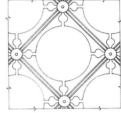

tetragonal four-fragment
linghua pattern

H-silworm pattern
brocade

square-lantern brocade

lantern brocade

lozenge

lozenge species

square in square

square-lantern
brocade

parallel-strip frame

ice-crack pattern

three-arrow pattern

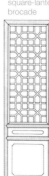

diagonal gammadion

orthogonal gammadion

zigzag brocade

turtle-back brocade

Waterside roofed walkways in the western part of Zhuozhengyuan Garden

The long walkway along the boundary wall runs in a northerly and southerly direction, crossing the lake. Its undulating form, the everchanging light cast through the decorative windows and the reverted images in the water are a wonderful sight.

Corridor bridge in Yuyin Shanfang (Mountain Villa with Ancestral Blessings)

The bridge corridor is located on the east edge of the lotus pond. Exquisitely built, it is typical of the architectural style of the Guangdong area. The building to the left of picture is the main building of the garden, Shenliu Tang (Hall in the Depth of Willows).

Xiaocangllangting (Small Surging Wave Pavilion), Yiyuan Garden

front elevation   section   circular plan

0 1 2 m

Taying Ting (Pavilion in Shadow of Pagoda), Zhuozhengyuan Garden

front elevation   section   circular plan

0 1 2 m

Yihong Ting (leaning against the Rainbow Pavilion), Zhuozhengyuan Garden

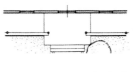

front elevation   section   circular plan

0 1 2 m

Xiuqi Ting (Pavilion of Unique Beauty), Zhuozhengyuan Garden

front elevation   section   circular plan

0 1 2

Li Ting (Bamboo-Hat Pavilion), Zhuozhengyuan Garden

front elevation

section

circular plan

Luyi Ting (Pavilion of Green Ripple), Zhuozhengyuan Garden

side elevation

section

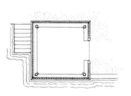

circular plan

Canglangting (Surging Wave Pavilion), Canglangting Garden

front elevation

section

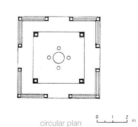

circular plan

Plan of roofed walkways

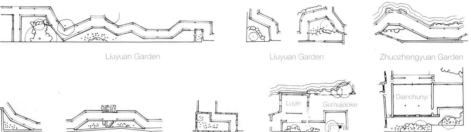

Liuyuan Garden

Liuyuan Garden

Zhuozhengyuan Garden

Luyin Gumujiaoke

Dianchunyi

Liuyuan Garden

Canglangting Garden

Liuyuan Garden

Wangshiyuan Garden

Section of roofed walkways

Xiaofeihong,
Zhuozhengyuan Garden

Winding roofed walkway,
Huafangzhai, Yiyuan Garden

Winding roofed walkway, Wufeng
Xianguan, Liuyuan Garden

Winding roofed walkway,
Yuedaofenglai Pavilion,
Wangshiyuan Garden

Liuyinluqu open
roofed walkway,
Zhuozhengyuan Garden

Yuancuige roofed
walkway, Liuyuan Garden

Lixuetang roofed
walkway, Shizilin Garden

Baishixuan parallel roofed
walkway, Yiyuan Garden

Parallel roofed walkway
at a small square hall,
Shizilin Garden

Roofed walkway over water, Zhuozhengyuan Garden

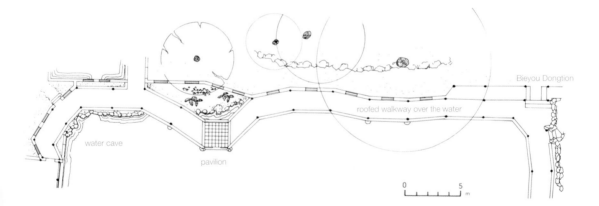

water cave

pavilion

Bieyou Dongtion

roofed walkway over the water

0   5
m

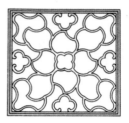

front walkway of Gumujiaoke,
Liuyuan Garden

front walkway of Gumujiaoke,
Liuyuan Garden

walkway in the northern yard,
Yanyu Hall, Shizilin Garden

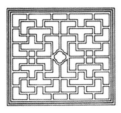

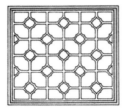

front walkway of Gumujiaoke,
Liuyuan Garden

front walkway of Gumujiaoke,
Liuyuan Garden

front walkway of Gumujiaoke,
Liuyuan Garden

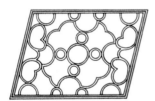

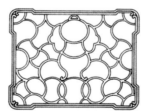

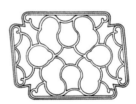

walkway the north of rockery,
Canglangting Garden

walkway the north of rockery,
Canglangting Garden

walkway the north of rockery,
Canglangting Garden

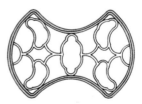

walkway the north of rockery,
Canglangting Garden

walkway the north of rockery,
Canglangting Garden

walkway the north of rockery,
Canglangting Garden'

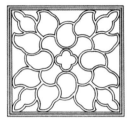

front walkway in the northern yard,
Yanyu Hall, Shizilin Garden

front walkway in the northern yard,
Yanyu Hall, Shizilin Garden

walkway the north of rockery,
Canglangting Garden

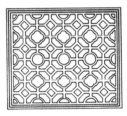

front walkway of Gumujiaoke,
Liuyuan Garden

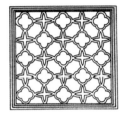

front walkway of Gumujiaoke,
Liuyuan Garden

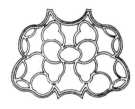

walkway the north of rockery,
Canglangting Garden

west walkway, Yaohua
Jingjie, Canglangting Garden

east walkway, Zhibai Xuan,
Shizilin Garden

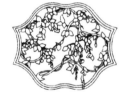

west walkway, Zhibai Xuan,
Shizilin Garden

walkway, to the rear of
Wenmei Ge, Shizilin Garden

east walkway, Yaohua Jingjie,
Canglangting Garden

east end of the north walkway,
Yanyu Hall, Shizilin Garden

walkway in the northern yard,
Yanyu Hall, Shizilin Garden

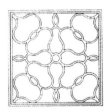

east end of the north walkway,
square hall, Shizilin Garden

The Excellence of Ancient Chinese Architecture

———————

Private Gardens

Notes on the Photographs

Gardens for the Enjoyment
of Artificial Landscapes of Men of Letters

China's private gardens are the artistic expression of an ancient hermit ideology. They underwent gradual change in the course of time — from the extensive to the compact, from the uncouth to the refined, and from the rough to the exquisite. In later feudal society, gardens became an ideal environment sought after by men of letters, as well as by rich merchants and aristocrats as lovers of cultural pursuits. The rich and fertile land south of the Yangtze River was a region which could boast the emergence of a great number of highly learned scholars, and consequently became a region where private gardens flourished. Suzhou is the city which prides itself in the greatest number of private gardens, which constitute the majority of those in this collection, the rest to be found in the cities of Nanjing, Shanghai, Yangzhou, and the Zhejiang and Guangdong provinces. Practically all the famous gardens existing in China today are included in this collection, and details have been given of their layout, building form and style. Readers are introduced to the unique techniques of building rockeries and treating water surfaces. The beauty of winding roofed walkways and perforated windows, the fascination of everchanging scenery, and the inventive artistry of borrowing views will all serve to acquaint the reader the unparalleled splendour of the private gardens in the southern parts of China.

Xiaofeihong (Little Flying Rainbow), Zhuozhengyuan Garden, Suzhou

Xiaofeihong (Little Flying Rainbow) is the most unique kind of roofed-walkway bridge ever built in Suzhou gardens. It is slightly curved, spanning the water so gracefully that it looks like a rainbow. Looking north from Xiaocanglangting (Small Surging-Wave Pavilion), one can see Songfeng Ting (Pavilion of Pine and Wind) to the right. Hefengsimian Ting (Pavilion with Lotus and Breezes on Four Sides), Jianshan Lou and Yiyu Xuan are all visible from the corridor bridge. By conveying a feeling of fathomlessness, the architect-gardener has here created a unique garden, in which one experiences the limitless within a limited space.

Daoying Lou (Storied Building with Inverted Reflection in Water) and outer wall of Zhuozhengyuan Garden (Humble Administrator's Garden), Suzhou / left

This building is located at the northern end of the lake in Buyuan Garden. The scenery here is mainly centered round the water. A winding roofed walkway was built by the lake along the boundary wall, its southern end leading to Yiliang Ting (Pavilion for Enjoying Scenery in Two Directions) and the northern end to Daoying Lou (Hall with Inverted Image in Water). The two buildings standing across the water set off one another. In the photograph, the building in the distance is Daoying Lou, and the whitewashed, evy-covered wall with its open-tracery windows was given the name of "cloud wall" on account of its undulating top.

Yuanxiang Tang (Hall of Distant Fragrance), Zhuozhengyuan Garden, Suzhou / right

Being the main building of the garden, Yuanxiang Tang (Hall of Distant Fragrance) is located centrally at a point where the scenery is at its best, with water, a bridge and luxuriant plantings of trees and flowers. It is a four-sided hall, the full-length lattice windows all offering different views: the terrace on the northern side an ideal vantage point for enjoying the lotus flowers; the trees, rockeries and flowers to the south beautiful to behold all year round; the pavilion to the east surrounded by trees and rare flowers and the veranda to its west picturesque with its intricate roofed walkway. As in a scroll painting, the artist has captured the feeling of wild nature and its ever-changing moods and seasons.

Xiangzhou (Fragrant Isle), Zhuozhengyuan Garden, Suzhou

Located to the west of Yuanxiang Tang, Xiangzhou (Fragrant Isle) is a boat-shaped building consisting of three elements. The front of the building faces east, its two sides bordering on water. The two-storied rear part is named Chengguan Lou (Lucid View Storied Building). Installed in the middle section of the "boat" is a large mirror, which draws into the building all the beautiful scenery on the east side of the lake.

Jianshan Lou (Storied Building with a View of Mountains), Zhuozhengyuan Garden, Suzhou

Located in the northwest part of the garden and surrounded by water, Jianshan Lou (Storied Building with a View of Mountains) is a comparatively large construction, which is connected with the other parts of the garden by a corridor bridge. It has a white marble podium. The first story of the building has open tracery windows, through which the scenery beyond is visible. The second story has white window screens which match well with the marble podium. Wide double eaves separate the upper and lower stories. On the west side, rocks are built into the rockery to serve as steps leading to the upper story, from which one can see the distant Tiger Hill Pagoda.

Scenery in the western section of Zhuozhengyuan Garden and the Beisi Ta (North Temple Pagoda), Suzhou

Standing on the island in the middle of the lake, Hefengsimian Ting (Pavilion with Lotus and Breezes on Four Sides) is surrounded by water on three sides. To its east is Xiangxue Yunwei Ting (Fragrant Snow and Colourful Clouds Pavilion), and to its south are Xiaofeihong, Xiaocanglangting and Xiangzhou. Across the water to the west lies the Bieyou Dongtian pavilion, and in the north, Jianshan Lou (Storied Building with a View of Mountains) is clearly visible. The pavilion is open on four sides, enabling the beautiful scenery all around to be appreciated. The Beisi Ta (North Temple Pagoda) in the distance is a perfect example of "borrowed view", illustrating the technique of creating scenery using "borrowed views" in Chinese garden architecture.

Bieyou Dongtian (Realm of Exceptional Beauty), Zhuozhengyuan Garden, Suzhou

Bieyou Dongtian (Realm of Exceptional Beauty) is a pavilion standing at the wall that divides the central and western sections of the garden. Nearby, weeping willows sway in the wind, and in the lake in front lotus flowers bloom in abundance. Against the whitewashed wall, they resemble a scene from a scroll painting. Within the pavilion, there is a moon-shaped door opening leading to the western section, the Buyuan Garden. On the pavilion there hangs a tablet inscribed with two Chinese characters, "Yong Cui", meaning "Embracing the Green", which became another name for the pavilion.

Liuyinluqu (Willow-shaded Winding Path), Zhuozhengyuan Garden, Suzhou

To the north of Bieyou Dongtian lies the winding roofed walkway Liuyinluqu (Willow-shaded Winding Path) with willow trees, bamboos and flowers planted on both sides. It is constructed of wood, and lanterns in subdued colours hang from its roof. The scenery changes at every turn.

Liuyinluqu viewed from Hefengsimian Ting (Pavilion with Lotus and Breezes on Four Sides), Zhuozhengyuan Garden, Suzhou

Looking west from Hefengsimian Ting (Pavilion with Lotus and Breezes on Four Sides), one can see a zigzag stone bridge spanning the lake almost touching the water, and connecting with the Liuyinluqu walkway on the other side. The lotus flowers in the lake, the willows on the bank and the stones lying by the side all create a beautiful setting. Behind the walkway is a stretch of luxurious green. This is a good example of the important role played by plants in creating a poetic ambiance and in sectoring spatial units.

Wuzhuyouju (Secluded Lodge amid Phoenix Trees and Bamboos), Zhuozhengyuan Garden, Suzhou

Wuzhuyouju (Secluded Lodge amid Phoenix Trees and Bamboos) is a pavilion located at the east end of the lake. It has moon-shaped doors installed on all four sides, and a veranda surrounding it. Through the moon-shaped door on the south side, one can see water, a bridge and Haitangchunwu (Spring Begonia Cove) in the distance. On the west side, Hefengsimian Ting (Pavilion with Lotus and Breezes on Four Sides) can be seen, and to the north stands Luyi Ting (Pavilion of Green Ripples). The boundary wall of the garden is on the east side of the pavilion, so that the moon-shaped opening on that side is actually a doorway, with bamboo and phoenix trees planted nearby.

Xuexiangyunwei Ting (Fragrant Snow and Colourful Clouds Pavilion), Zhuozhengyuan Garden, Suzhou

Sitting on top of the main peak of the rockery, Xuexiangyunwei Ting (Fragrant Snow and Colourful Clouds Pavilion) looks across the water to Yuanxiang Tang Hall. It is a rectangular-shaped pavilion with a front terrace extending to the edge of the cliff. From here a panoramic view of the whole garden can be enjoyed. There is a couplet carved on the columns of the pavilion, an example of the calligraphy of the famous Ming scholar Wen Zhengming.

Xiuqi Ting (Pavilion of Unique Beauty), Zhuozhengyuan Garden, Suzhou

Xiuqi Ting (Pavilion of Unique Beauty) is located on an artificial hill to the east of Yuanxiang Tang, north of Pipa Yuan, and to the west of Haitangchunwu. It is surrounded by an abundance of peonies, so that it looks especially colourful in spring when the flowers are in bloom. Gigantic trees growing in profusion on its north side cast deep shade over the pavilion. The small path leading up to it is paved with moss-covered rocks. In the interior there is a tablet hung in the middle of the beam, and a couplet is inscribed on two columns.

Haitangchunwu (Spring Begonia Cove), Zhuozhengyuan Garden, Suzhou

Located to the east of Xiuqi Ting (Pavilion of Unique Beauty), Haitangchunwu (Spring Begonia Cove) is a small enclosed courtyard, only 130 square meters large. The house has only two bays widthwise, and is used as a study. Begonia trees are planted in the yard, and combined with bamboos and stones. The ground is paved with pebbles in yellow, white and blue arranged in the shape of begonia flowers. The atmosphere in this charming little courtyard is one of utmost tranquility.

The winding roofed walkway of Jianshan Lou, Zhuozhengyuan Garden, Suzhou

The winding roofed walkway is well planned and of superb craftsmanship. The inverted image of the walkway, the greenery all around and the white clouds in the blue sky form a perfect setting. The scenery on the other side of the white wall is only partly visible through the casementless windows.

Winding roofed walkway and Yiliang Ting, Zhuozhengyuan Garden, Suzhou

The winding roofed walkway has water on one side, and trees on the other. The lush trees ward off the heat on summer days. The water twists and turns with the winding walkway. The open tracery windows along the wall show a great diversity of patterns, and allow the scenery beyond to be only partly visible. The combination of wall and open tracery windows not only adds beauty but also sections off the space.

Scenery of the garden viewed from Yiliang Ting (Pavilion for Enjoying Scenery in Two Directions), Zhuozhengyuan Garden, Suzhou

Yiliang Ting (Pavilion for Enjoying Scenery in Two Directions) is in the Buyuan Garden. From here, one can see Daoying Lou to the north across the lake, Sanshiliu Yuanyang Guan (Thirty-six Mandarin Ducks Hall) and Shiba Mantuoluo Guan (Eighteen Camellia Hall) in the west. Lotus grows in the pond and a bridge spans the water. The pavilion is surrounded by greenery and made attractive by moss-covered rockeries.

Pipa Yuan (Loquat Orchard), Zhuozhengyuan Garden, Suzhou

The Pipa Yuan (Loquat Orchard) in an independent courtyard in the southeast corner of the garden, with Linglong Guan and Jiashi Ting standing close. Loquat trees are widely planted in the yard. The undulating wall on the west side ending at the foot of the rockery separates the yard from the principal scenic area in the garden. The moon gate entrance in the wall serves to frame the scenery, and the pavilion on the artificial hill in the distance can just be seen. It is a typical example of "view borrowing". The ground in the courtyard is paved with pebbles arranged in ice-crack patterns. Xiuqi Ting to the north of the courtyard becomes a scenic focal point.

EXAMPLES OF PAVEMENTS

Liuyuan Garden

Liuyuan Garden

Shizilin Garden

Liuyuan Garden

Liuyuan Garden

Shizilin Garden

Liuyuan Garden

Liuyuan Garden

Yiyuan Garden

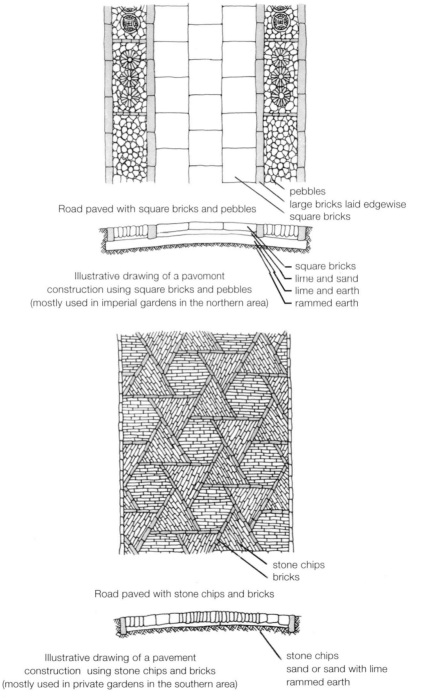

Road paved with square bricks and pebbles

pebbles
large bricks laid edgewise
square bricks

Illustrative drawing of a pavomont
construction using square bricks and pebbles
(mostly used in imperial gardens in the northern area)

square bricks
lime and sand
lime and earth
rammed earth

stone chips
bricks

Road paved with stone chips and bricks

Illustrative drawing of a pavement
construction using stone chips and bricks
(mostly used in private gardens in the southern area)

stone chips
sand or sand with lime
rammed earth

117

Interior view of the north hall in Sanshiliu Yuanyang Guan (Thirty-six Mandarin Ducks Hall), Zhuozhengyuan Garden, Suzhou

Sanshiliu Yuanyang Guan (Thirty-Six Mandarin Ducks Hall) is located at the southern end of the lake in Buyuan Garden, with Yiliang Ting to its east and Liuting Ge to its west. A tablet hung high on the beam bears the name of the hall is in beautiful calligraphy. The building has exquisitely shaped windows, which provide good lighting, and contains fine old pieces of furniture. Sanshiliu Yuanyang Guan is an excellent example of the beauty of Chinese classical architecture with its beam and column structure, the way its windows are used for light, the design of the furniture, and the treatment of its internal space.

Yushuitongzuo Xuan, Zhuozhengyuan Garden, Suzhou

Located in an attractive setting in the central part of the west garden, Yushuitongzuo Xuan is also referred to as fan-shaped pavilion or bamboo-hat pavilion. Standing on the waterside, it is fan-shaped in plan, of exquisite construction, the side facing east is open, whereas the other three sides are all provided with walls that have interestingly shaped window openings. The stone table, stools and chairs in the pavilion are all fan-shaped.

Fan-shaped windows of Yushuitongzuo Xuan (Whom-to-sit-with Pavilion), Zhouzhengyuan Garden, Suzhou

This picture is taken in Yushuitongzuo Xuan (Whom-to-sit-with Pavilion). Looking eastwards through the fan-shaped window opening, one can see Bieyou Dongtian in the distance. Doors and windows play an important role in Chinese architecture, especially garden architecture. The shapes of the openings often provides an attractive feature, and "framing the scenery" is one of the well-established principles, in that by "borrowing views" one has the impression of experiencing the limitless in a limited space.

Daoying Lou (Storied Building with Inverted Reflection in Water), Zhuozhengyuan Garden, Suzhou

Daoying Lou (Storied Building with Inverted Reflection in Water) is located in the western part of the Buyuan Garden. Situated at the lakeside, it is the finest building in this part of Zhuozhengyuan Garden. The ground floor of the building is also named Baiwen Yishen Zhizhai (Study in Honour of Wen and Shen), Wen being Wen Zhengming and Shen, Shen Shitian of the Ming Dynasty. The stone carvings of the images of the two famous scholars and Wen Zhengming's essay Record of the Zhuozhengyuan Garden of the Wang Family are mounted on the wall.

Sanshiliu Yuanyang Guan, Zhuozhengyuan Garden, Suzhou

Being the main building in Buyuan Garden, this hall used to be the place where the owners of the garden, the Zhang family, carried out most of their important activities. The north side of the hall is built onto the water and supported by strong wooden poles. The hall, square in shape, is divided by partitions into front and back sections, the front one bearing the name of the Thirty-six Mandarin Ducks Hall, while the rear, the Eighteen Camellia Hall. In the old days, eighteen camellia trees stood in front of the hall, and mandarin ducks were kept in the lake, hence the name.

Xiuzhu Ge (Pavilion of Slender Bamboos), Shizilin Garden, Suzhou

Located to the south of the eastern rockery, Xiuzhu Ge (Pavilion of Slender Bamboos) is built across the water, and is open on both the north and south sides. Its name derives from the bamboos planted around. The old bamboo groves are still well kept today, and more flowers and trees have been newly planted in the vicinity.

Shan Ting (Fan Pavilion) in Shizilin Garden (Lion Grove Garden), Suzhou
opposite page

Sited at the corner of the wall in the southwestern part of the garden, this is again a fan-shaped pavilion. Since it is located high up on a rockery, standing in the pavilion is like standing on a precipice overlooking a deep pool. On the back wall of the building, there is a fan-shaped window opening, through which the rockeries and bamboos in a tiny yard to the rear can be seen as if in a painting. This pavilion is small, but refined and exquisitely built.

Chengqu Caotang (City Corner Thatched Cottage) in Ouyuan Garden (Twin Garden), Suzhou

Chengqu Caotang (City Corner Thatched Cottage) is the main hall in the eastern part of the garden, which used to be Lu Jing's private garden. Towards the end of the Qing Dynasty, it was transferred to Shen Bingcheng, who invited a painter to do the planning for the garden, and this is how it looks today. The hall, two-storied and double-eaved, is located in the north of the garden. The first floor has three bays widthwise, and on the second story there is a parallel roofed walkway leading to the residential mansion, a design unique in the gardens in Suzhou. In front of the building, there is a spacious courtyard provided with stone tables and chairs, and to the side, stands a yellow stone high rockery of super craftsmanship.

Shanshuijian (Pavilion amid Hills and Water), Ouyuan Garden, Suzhou

Shanshuijian (Pavilion amid Hills and Water) is an open waterside pavilion in the center of the lake. Water lies on the north and south sides of the pavilion, and rockeries on the east and west sides, conveying a feeling of being amid water and hills. A small zigzag bridge crosses the water not far from the pavilion, and plants grow in profusion all around.

Wu'ai Ting (Pavilion I Love) and winding roofed walk way, Ouyuan Garden, Suzhou

Ouyuan Garden, located in Xiaoxinqiao Lane in Suzhou, was first built during the Qing Dynasty. Wu'ai Ting (Pavilion I Love) sits on top of the high rockery in the southeastern part of the garden. Sitting in the pavilion, one can see Chengqu Caotang to the north, Shanshuijian to the west and Tinglu Lou to the south. The rockery is built of yellow stones. The small bridge zigzags its way across the lake, thus allowing different views to be had as one walks along.

Interior view of Wanjuan Tang (Hall of Ten-Thousand Books), Wangshiyuan Garden, Suzhou

The Wangshiyuan Garden is made up of the east and west sections, the east being the residential quarter and the west the garden. The main hall, Wanjuan Tang, is arranged on the central axis after the main entrance gate and the sedan-chair hall. The paintings, calligraphy, couplets, furniture, and even the rear windows and the lanterns hung from the beams are all arranged symmetrically. Nothing in the hall is luxurious or sophisticated, but old, refined and subdued in colour. In the center of the hall, there is a painting of an ancient pine tree, the pine, according to Chinese tradition, being a symbol of high moral integrity.

Interior view of Xiexiu Lou (Storied Building for Gathering Beautiful Scenery), Wangshiyuan Garden, Suzhou

Xiexiu Lou (Storied Building for Gathering Beautiful Scenery) in the residential quarter is an inner hall for receiving lady guests. There are beautiful brick carvings on the lintel. The utilization of space, the grouping of furniture, the arrangement of doors and windows, and even the use of colour all give an insight into how people of the time might have lived. The gable wall of this building is almost on the verge of the lake, where there are rockeries and a wisteria trellis.

Zhusongchengmao Men (Gate of Luxuriant Bamboos and Pines), Wangshiyuan Garden, Suzhou

Wangshiyuan Garden is small, but its layout, scenery and architectural details were all planned with careful deliberation. The picture here shows the gate between the main and the inner hall. Its design is quite different from gates in general. It has a single course of dougong, an exquisitely carved beam and beautiful brick carvings. The name of the gate Zhusongchengmao Men (Gate of Luxuriant Bamboos and Pines) is written in four large characters on the lintel, decorated with two elegantly carved bricks on each side.

Zaoyao Gaoxiang Men (Shining Brightly and Rising High Gate), Wangshiyuan Garden (Retired Fisherman's Garden), Suzhou / opposite page

Wangshiyuan Garden is situated on the southern side of Youyi Road in Suzhou. It was the original site of Shi Zhengzhi's Wanjuan Tang (Hall of Ten Thousand Books) built during the Southern Song Dynasty, restored during the Qianlong reign of the Qing Dynasty. Shown in the picture is the north gate of the sedan-chair hall, leading to the main hall. This gate with exquisite brick carvings has a remarkable dougong structure and is unique in design. A tablet inscribed with handsome calligraphy hangs in the center of the gateway and bears its name Zaoyao Gaoxiang Men (Shining Brightly and Rising High Gate). The plain white wall serves as a foil to the gate.

Scenery along the northeastern side of the lake, Wangshiyuan Garden, Suzhou

In the picture, the building bordering on the water is Zhuwaiyizhi Xuan (Veranda of the Slanting Bamboo Twig). With Jixu Zhai (Study of the Ethereal) in the north as a foil, it has a homely look about it. To the east of the veranda is Wufeng Shuwu (Five-Peaks Study) and an artificial hill. The building to the west of Jixu Zhai is Kansongduhua Xuan (Veranda for Enjoying Pine Trees and Deriving Joy from Paintings), which has pines, plum trees and maples planted around it.

Zhuoying Shuige viewed from Qiaofengjing (Woodcutter's Path), Wangshiyuan Garden, Suzhou

The waterside pavilion Zhuoying Shuige is built on the southern shore of the lake. Seats with balustrades line the side bordering on the water. To the east of the building there is a rockery of yellow stones. The roofed walkway on its west side has a zigzag shape, and so the views presented to the visitor vary at every turn. The building has an outward appearance that is simple and unadorned. It is open on the side facing the lake, and so is a good place to enjoy the beautiful scenery and light breezes.

Tiyunshi Courtyard (Serried Clouds Chamber), Wangshiyuan Garden, Suzhou

Located in the northeast corner of the garden, Tiyunshi (Serried Clouds Chamber) is the first building one would see when using the rear door entrance. The rockery, of carefully chosen stones, are perfect examples of the art, and even the plants among the rocks have been carefully selected so that different colours of flowers and leaves can be enjoyed all year round. When the morning sun shines on the plants, the shadow they cast on the whitewashed wall resembles a Chinese painting on white paper. The pattern of the pavement is simple and elegant, on a par with the beauty of the courtyard.

Stone yard in Tiyunshi Courtyard, Wangshiyuan Garden, Suzhou

Stone was considered an important element in the creation of landscape not only in gardens, but in small courtyards as well. It was held that "A garden can do without artificial hills, but not without stones", and that "Trees can fully unfold their beauty only when they are set off by stones; and stones cannot display their power and strength without trees." The rockeries in the courtyard outside Tiyunshi (Serried Cloud Chamber) show admirable craftsmanship, and are enlivened by the trees and grass grown among the rocks. The patterns of pebble paving are also highly innovative.

Side gate of Wufeng Shuwu (Five-Peak Study), Wangshiyuan Garden, Suzhou

Wufeng Shuwu (Five-Peaks Study) is in the northeastern part of the garden. To its west are Jixu Zhai and Zhuwaiyizhi Xuan. Further on, one can see Sheya Lang (Duck-Shooting Roofed Walkway) and Xiexiu Lou (Storied Building for Gathering Beautiful Scenery) in front of it. If one looks behind, one will see Tiyunshi (Serried Clouds Chamber) to the rear. The study is connected with the moon-shaped entrance gate of Tiyunshi. Its side gate has slender and highly upturned roof ridges. Trees and flowers are planted in abundance round the building, and the rockeries are especially remarkable.

Xiaoshanchonggui Xuan (Studio of Sweet Osmanthus Hillock), Wangshiyuan Garden, Suzhou

Located to the south of the lake, Xiaoshanchonggui Xuan (Hall of Sweet Osmanthus Hillock) is open on four sides to facilitate enjoyment of the surrounding scenery. A winding roofed walkway connects the hall with the waterside pavilion, Zhuoying Shuige. By the side of it stands a rockery of yellow stones, not large or intricate, but nevertheless grand and powerful, and displaying fine craftsmanship. On its left is a bridge, which greatly enhances the scenery.

Sheyalang (Duck-shooting Roofed Walkway), Wangshiyuan Garden, Suzhou

Located on the east side of the lake, Sheya Lang (Duck-shooting Roofed Walkway) looks across the water to Yuedaofenglai Ting (Pavilion Welcoming the Advent of Moon and Breezes) on the west side. All the buildings in Wangshiyuan Garden are exquisitely built, and all different. The winding walkway has delicately curved roof ridges, forming a contrast with the sturdy columns and beams. The scenery round the walkway is fascinating with weeping willows, blossoming lotus flowers and trees casting a deep shade. On autumn evenings, it is also an ideal place for enjoying the moon.

Zhuoying Shuige (Tassel-Washing Waterside Pavilion) viewed from Zhuwaiyizhi Xuan (Veranda outside a Slanting Bamboo Twig), Wangshiyuan Garden, Suzhou

Zhuwaiyizhi Xuan (Veranda of the Slanting Bamboo Twig), sitting amid trees, bamboos, stones and water, is located at an exceptionally beautiful spot on the northeastern side of the lake, and one can look from here through a moon-shaped door opening to Zhuoying Shuige (Tassel-Washing Waterside Pavilion) across the water. The design of the moon-shaped door opening is simple, but the scenery beyond, with green plants, rockeries and water is enchanting. This view is a good illustration of the role played by door or window openings in Chinese gardens.

Door of Kansongduhua Xuan (Veranda for Enjoying Pine Trees and Deriving Joy from Paintings), Wangshiyuan Garden, Suzhou

One of the important buildings on the north side of the lake, Kansongduhua Xuan (Veranda for Enjoying Pine Trees and Deriving Joy from Paintings) is a studio sited in a quiet environment. Its furnishing is elegant and refined. In the courtyard outside, there are ancient trees such as lacebark pines, cypresses, sweet osmanthus, as well as peonies and winter sweets. The full-length doors in the picture are on the southern side of the studio. They provide the house with good lighting and ventilation, and through them the small bridge, running water, whitewashed walls and a profusion of greenery can all be seen.

Scenery seen through the windows of Dianchunyi (Late Spring Study), Wangshiyuan Garden, Suzhou

Dianchunyi (Late Spring Study), an exquisite independent courtyard in the northwest corner of the garden, has rockeries, trees and flowers arranged against the wall on three sides. In the past, herbaceous peony used to be planted in the yard. The study is thus named because the plant blossoms in late spring. The windows shown in the picture face a narrow strip of land to the north, planted with bamboos and banana trees and decorated with rockeries. The highly decorative windows with lace-like patterns frame the view outside, making the whole look like a delicate Chinese watercolour painting. Ming Xuan, built in 1979 in the Metropolitan Museum in New York, was modeled on Dianchunyi.

Yuedaofenglai Ting (Pavilion Welcoming the Advent of the Moon and Breezes), Wangshiyuan Garden, Suzhou

Standing at the west end of the lake and looking across the water to Sheyalang, Yuedaofenglai Ting (Pavilion Welcoming the Advent of the Moon and Breezes) is built on the rocks by the side of the lake. The winding roofed walkway and bridge to the rear lead to Zhuwaiyizhi Xuan and Zhuoying Shuige. The design of the pavilion is unique, with its top rising high, and its roof ridges curving elegantly. Seats with balustrades are installed between the columns.

Wall and shadows of trees in front of Lengquan Ting (Cold Spring Pavilion), Wangshiyuan Garden, Suzhou

Walls play an important role in garden design, providing spatial division and preventing direct views. They can serve as routes through the garden as well. The scenes seen through the open tracery windows on the wall tend to arouse the curiosity of the viewer. The shadows cast by the sun on the whitewashed walls, sometimes vague, sometimes substantial, recall Chinese ink-and-wash paintings. The wall shown in the picture is that in front of Lengquan Ting (Cold Spring Pavilion), located to the west of Dianchunyi.

Gate of Canglangting Garden (Surging Wave Pavilion Garden), Suzhou

Canglangting (Surging-Wave Pavilion Garden) is a garden that has water outside its boundary and hills inside. Located on the southern bank of a river, one first sees pavilions and rockeries at the water's edge before entering the garden. Passing through the garden gate and crossing the stone bridge, one then sees beautiful rockeries in front of one. Although this famous garden has experienced neglect as well as periods of prosperity, it has succeeded in preserving its traditional appearance to the present day. Lying in the deep shade of ancient trees, the garden, with its long winding roofed walkways and pavilions with superb upward-curving roof ridges, is a place to enjoy the cool in summer time.

Canglangting (Surging Wave Pavilion), Canglangting Garden, Suzhou
opposite page

Canglangting (Surging-Wave Pavilion) sits on the ridge of the eastern section of the rockery hill. It is built of stone beams and columns, looking old and elegant, and has a couplet written in gracious calligraphy carved on two columns. A stone table and stools are installed in the pavilion. From there, one can have a panoramic view of the garden. The attraction of the scenery in this garden lies more in natural beauty than in artificial craftsmanship.

Interior view of Ouxiang Xie (Fragrant Lotus Root Waterside Pavilion) in Yiyuan Garden (Delightful Garden), Suzhou

Situated on the west side of Renmin Street in Suzhou, Yiyuan Garden was built later than any of the other gardens there. It therefore had the advantage of being able to absorb the merits of other gardens in its layout. Located on the southern side of the lake in the western section of the garden, Ouxiang Xie (Fragrant Lotus Root Waterside Pavilion) is sometimes also called Lotus Flower Hall. It is furnished in a simple and elegant style. The windows with their decorative surrounds are large, allowing the scenery to be clearly seen. This waterside pavilion is constructed in the style of a mandarin-duck hall, the northern part for enjoying the lotus flowers in the lake, the southern part for taking delight in the moon.

Parallel Roofed Walkway, Yiyuan Garden, Suzhou

Yiyuan Garden is made up of two distinct parts, the eastern part and the western one, the parallel roofed walkway being the division line between the two. The eastern section was the original mansion of a Ming Dynasty minister, and was subsequently divided up into several courtyards. The western section was a later development, and forms a contrast to the earlier part in that a lake and hills are its dominant features, whereas the eastern part consists mainly of buildings. By arranging a parallel roofed walkway with open tracery windows between the two parts, each section benefits from the merits of the other; and each becomes the "borrowed view" of the other.

Cilu Men (Cilu Gate), Yipu Garden (Art Orchard), Suzhou

Located in Wenya Lane in Suzhou, Yipu Garden used to be a garden for growing medicinal herbs, and belonged to the Wen family, who lived during the Ming Dynasty. Extending over 3,000 square meters, a lake forms the centerpiece, with most of the buildings located to its north. On the southern side of the lake, there are artificial hills and an abundance of trees. Pavilions, roofed walkways and waterside verandas are built on the east and west sides of the lake. In the southwest corner, there is an independent courtyard enclosed by walls. Cilu Men (Cilu Gate) is the moon-gate entrance to the small yard.

Yu'ou Men (Gate of the Bathing Gull), Yipu Garden, Suzhou

Yu'ou Men (Gate of the Bathing Gull) is another moon-gate entrance to a secluded courtyard to the southeast of the lake. The name of the gate is carved on the stone tablet above the gateway. Ivy covers the wall, and a formidable-looking rockery stands by the gate. The courtyard is paved with tiny pebbles. Through the moon-gate entrance, the other moon-shaped door opening, the Cilu Gate, is visible. Stones, water, a small bridge, trees and flowers fill the space between the two door openings, which thus become a "borrowed view" for each other, an innovative "view borrowing" treatment.

Casementless windows at Gumujiaoke (Intertwined Old Trees), Liuyuan Garden (Lingering Garden), Suzhou

First built during the Ming Dynasty, the garden is located outside the Changmen Gate in Suzhou. In spite of the fact that over the centuries it witnessed both war and the changes in ownership, it fortunately escaped destruction. "Liu" in Chinese means "to remain" or "to linger"; and the family name of a one-time owner of the garden had the same sound "Liu", and so the garden was given its name. Gumujiaoke (Intertwined Old Trees) is one of the eighteen outstanding scenic spots, and the first the visitor sees on entering the garden. Winding roofed walkways are used to form several small courtyards, and the open tracery windows on the walls result in an innovative treatment of space. The scenery in the garden is only partly to be seen through the traceries, thus forming just the prelude to the magnificent view that is later visible.

Huabu Xiaozhu (Huabu Garden Furnishing), Liuyuan Garden, Suzhou
opposite page

This is a tiny narrow yard to the south of Luyin Xuan. By arranging rocks, stone bamboo, bamboo and ivy against the whitewashed wall, a lively effect has been created. Liuyuan is not a large garden, but the buildings are numerous and comparatively large. Any feeling of congestion is relieved by the alternate use of large and small spatial units, Huabu Xiaozhu (Huabu garden furnishing) being an example.

Mingse Lou (Bright Zither Storied Hall), Liuyuan Garden, Suzhou

Mingse Lou (Bright Zither Storied Hall) is one of the important buildings in the garden. Standing on the southern side of the lake and connected with the Hanbi Shanfang (Cold Emerald Green Mountain Villa), it faces the main scenery to the north. There is no staircase in the building, and access to the upper storey is provided by steps through the rockery, a device often employed in gardens. The brick window frames, latticework, wooden balustrades and chairs on the second storey are all of exquisite design. The trees planted round the building are well chosen, and the tall green maple tree standing in front adds particularly to the exquisite charm of the building.

Wufeng Xianguan (Five-Peak Celestial Hall), Liuyuan Garden, Suzhou

Located in the eastern part, Wufeng Xianguan (Five-Peak Celestial Hall) is the main building in the group of halls in the center of the garden. Interestingly shaped stones, set among trees and bamboo groves, serve as its scenic focal point both in front and to the rear. There are two groups of small courtyards on its east side, used as studies or rooms for receiving guests. The yards, though small, are planted with precious trees such as ginko, camphor and magnolia, and decorated with Taihu stones. The name of the hall derives from the five peaks in the Lushan mountains referred to in a poem by the famous Tang poet Li Bai.

Ke Ting (Ke Pavilion), Liuyuan Garden, Suzhou

Standing on the artificial hill to the north of the lake, Ke Ting (Ke Pavilion) looks over to Mingse Lou and Hanbi Shanfang across the water, and is accessible by the steps leading through the rocks. Hexagonal in plan, it has six high upturned roof ridges, and lies deep in the shade of ancient trees that grow all over the hill. Sitting in the pavilion, one has before one a lovely setting comprising the lake and hills, the trees and flowers and the buildings.

Qingfengchiguan (Guest House of the Pond of Light Breezes), Liuyuan Garden, Suzhou / opposite page

Qingfengchiguan (Guest House of the Pond of Light Breezes) is located to the east of the lake, looking across the water to Wenmuxixiang Xuan (Veranda for Smelling the Fragrance of Sweet-Scented Osmanthus). The west side of the waterside pavilion is completely open allowing the scenery to be enjoyed to the full. Taihu stones, orchards and bamboo are a decorative feature, and to the rear are tall shady trees. An antique-looking stone pillar with a Buddhist inscription stands in the lake nearby, adding a touch of the venerable to this part of the garden. The two-storied building on the right of the picture is Xi Lou (West Storied Building).

Quxi Lou (Intricate Vale Storied Hall), Liuyuan Garden, Suzhou

Quxi Lou (Intricate Vale Storied Building) to the east of the lake adjoins the west building. There is a winding roofed corridor to its south leading to Gumujiaoke, and it has Mingse Lou across the lake to the west. It comprises five bays across, but is only 3 meters deep. Being neither a walkway nor a proper building for residence, its real function lies in the way it divides up the space and prevents a direct view. Located at the junction of garden and residence, it acts as a screen for the private quarters of the house. It is an attractive building with a superb upward-turning roof, and beautiful open tracery windows. Its main gate is octagonal in shape.

Quxi Lou (Intricate Vale Storied Hall), Liuyuan Garden, Suzhou / opposite page

This picture of Quxi Lou is taken from another angle. In the old days, there used to be two gigantic trees in front of the building, but they perished some years ago. The two small trees have been planted in their stead. The antique-looking stone pillar carved with Buddhist inscription is also visible in the picture.

Interior view of Wufeng Xianguan, Liuyuan Garden, Suzhou / preceding page

Wufeng Xianguan and the courtyards in its vicinity is where all the daily activities of the master of the garden used to take place. The hall is lofty and spacious, and the beams and columns all of the precious Nanmu wood, which emits a faint fragrant scent. It is, therefore, popularly referred to as the Nanmu Hall. The furnishings are extremely elegant and refined, with scroll paintings and calligraphy, a potted miniature landscape, exquisite tables and chairs and articles of daily use. A large tablet carved with the name of the hall is hung high up in the center. This is the largest hall in the gardens of Suzhou, and a place where one can strongly sense the "fragrance of books."

Corridor on the west side of Linquanqishuozhi Guan (Hall for the Venerable Elderly), Liuyuan Garden, Suzhou

Linquanqishuozhi Guan (Hall for the Venerable Elderly) is the most magnificent of the few grand halls in the gardens of Suzhou. The hanging fascia and openwork screen, the long, half and down-to-floor windows and latticework are of unparalleled beauty. In the corridor on the west side of the hall, there is a moon-gate entrance, through which the scenery outside can be glimpsed. On the inner side of the corridor, there is a vase-shaped window through which the interior of the hall can be discerned. Its walls are not built up to the eaves, the space left between serving ventilation and lighting purposes.

Winding roofed walkway on the west side of Guanyun Lou (Cloud-Capped Storied Building), Liuyuan Garden, Suzhou

Guanyun Lou (Cloud-Capped Storied Building) is in the courtyard to the west of Linquanqishuozhi Guan, and is where a 6.5m tall Taihu rock stands, the largest in the gardens of Suzhou. The winding roofed walkway is in the courtyard to the west of Guanyun Lou. The function of walkways in general is to serve as a covered route through the garden, to facilitate view borrowing and to enhance the artistic quality of the garden. As this one winds its way through the garden, the view presented to the visitor varies as he moves along. Walkways in gardens are thus always carefully designed, this one being a typical example.

Guyushenliang (Cold Rain on Mushrooms), Changqiao (Long Bridge) and Xintai Platform in Tuisiyuan Garden (Garden of Retreat and Contemplation), Wujiang

Built during the Guangxu reign of the Qing Dynasty, the garden used to be the residence of a high-ranking officer. Naohongyige is a land boat on the west side of the lake. Its terrace bordering on the water is an ideal place for taking delight in watching the fish swim about in the water. Guyushenliang (Cold Rain on Mushrooms) is a small waterside pavilion to the south of the lake. Steps through the rocks outside the building provide access to the upper story, from which an overall view of the garden can be had. Tuisiyuan is small, but it is an intimate garden following the well-established principles of the garden art.

Naohongyige (Big Land Boat) and Shuixiang Xie (Fragrant Water Waterside Pavilion), Tuisiyuan Garden, Wujiang

Naohongyige (Big Land Boat) is practically built over the water. It looks northwards over the lake to the Tuisi Caotang (Thatched Cottage for Retreat and Meditation) which also hugs the water. The small Shuixiang Xie (Fragrant Water Waterside Pavilion) stands between the two buildings, adding variety to the group. Rich plantings and beautifully-formed rocks provide decorative elements. Tuisiyuan Garden is located in Tongli in Wujiang County, in the province of Jiangsu. It, and the gardens of Suzhou, represent China's most outstanding group of private gardens.

Jingmiao Tang (Hall of Superb Quietude), Zhanyuan Garden, Nanjing

Jingmiao Tang (Hall of Superb Quietude), a flowery hall and the center of Zhanyuan Garden, was renovated during the Tongzhi reign (1862-1874) of the Qing Dynasty. The other buildings, including pavilions, roofed walkways and verandas as well as the artificial hill in the southern part of the garden, were all rebuilt or added in later years. On both the northern and southern sides of the hall, there are hills and lakes, and to the east of the lake is a winding roofed walkway and a small courtyard. On the west side, there is an artificial hill built of earth, where trees grow in profusion. The scenery on the northern side is more open, and there is a lawn in front of the hall. The lake is smaller on the southern side, and the front part of the hall facing the lake takes the form of a waterside veranda and seating with balustrades arranged between columns. The interior is elegantly decorated in the mandarin-duck hall style.

South rockery and pool in Zhanyuan Garden, Nanjing / left

The rockery is built entirely of Taihu rocks and boasts precipices, cliffs, overhanging rocks, stalactites, paths, grottos and waterfalls. Plants grow abundantly all over the rockery, lending it natural beauty. In the lake in front, stones are arranged to project over the water surface. The rockery faces north, and stands in perfect spatial relationship to the waterside veranda in front of Jingmiao Tang. The rockery was built in as recently as the 1970s.

Scenery in the garden viewed southward from the east side of the north rockery in Zhanyuan Garden (Looking-into-the-Distance Garden), Nanjing / right

Zhanyuan Garden (Looking-into-the-Distance Garden), located on Zhanyuan Road in Nanjing, was originally the residence of Xu Da, a general in the army of the first Ming emperor. Emperor Qianlong of Qing once visited it and gave it its current name. It was not until the Jiaqing reign of Qing that the place was turned into a garden. The rich planting on the high rockery on the northern side of the lake creates a feeling of wilderness. On the side of the rockery bordering on the lake, stones lie close to and parallel with the surface of the water, and connect with the stone bridge leading to other parts of the garden. The contrast formed by the vertical arrangement of the rockery and the horizontal stones at the water's edge was one of the characteristics of rockery design. A scene often depicted in classical Chinese landscape paintings was that of a man sitting fishing on stones that reached out into water, with the steep rockery behind him.

Zhiyujian (Fish-Knowing Balustrade) in Jichangyuan Garden (Garden to the Heart's Content), Wuxi

This garden lies at the foot of Huishan Hill in the western suburb of the city of Wuxi. It was first built by a court minister Qin Jin during the Zhengde reign (1506-1512) of the Ming Dynasty. Zhiyujian (Fish-Knowing Balustrade) is a pavilion built over the water. Together with winding roofed walkways, whitewashed walls, open tracery windows and waterside pavilions, it forms part of the scenery on the east bank of the lake. It looks across the water to the artificial hill on the western side of the lake, and Huishan Hill can be seen in the distance. The name Fish-Knowing Balustrade derives from the story of the Taoist philosopher Zhuang Zi discussing the happiness of the fish with his friend.

Scenery in the garden viewed southward from Jinghuiyi (Pool of Brocade-like Ripples), Jichangyuan Garden, Wuxi

The lake Jinghuiyi (Pool of Brocade-like Ripples) and the scenery around form the centerpiece of the garden. The lake, covering about 1,600 square meters in area, is of a narrow shape. It narrows even further in the middle, with Hebutan (Beach where Cranes Walk) on the west and Zhiyujian on the east. On the eastern side of the water there is a zigzag bridge of marble slabs hugging the surface. In the northeast corner, a corridor bridge obscures the end of the lake, creating the illusion that the stretch of water continues. Xishan Hill and the pagoda on its top are drawn into the garden as a borrowed view--- a classical example of view borrowing in Chinese garden design.

Yiyu Xuan, Geyuan Garden, Yangzhou

Yiyu Xuan (Hall for Pleasant Rain) is the main building in the garden, and was where all the daily activities took place. It is a four-sided hall, with full-length windows on all sides, and a veranda on three. The marble-lined walls on the east and west sides have been given flowery windows. The hall is magnificently furnished, and the space divided by an openwork screen installed between two columns. In front of the hall is a yard filled with trees and flowers, and the lake lies to the rear. To the east of the building is the yellow stone rockery, and to its west there used to be pavilions and roofed walkways, which now no longer exist. The roof of the hall is a single-eaved, hip-and-gable construction. Instead of being dramatically upturned, the roof ridges curve gently upwards, suggesting a mixture of northern and southern architectural styles

Rockery hill built with Taihu stones, Geyuan Garden, Yangzhou

This rockery by the side of the lake is built entirely of Taihu stones, and water flows into the grotto at its foot. The caves in the rockery are built so intricately that one has the sense of being in a labyrinth unable to find one's way out. Stone tables, stools and a stone bed are installed in the cave, suggesting that this is a haunt of fairies. The small square pavilion on top of the rockery is named He Ting (Crane Pavilion), and from here one has a panoramic view of the garden. The ancient tree standing by the pavilion casts a deep shadow over the hill. This is the so-called Summer Mountain in Geyuan Garden.

Fang Ting (Square Pavilion), Heyuan Garden, Yangzhou

Fang Ting (Square Pavilion) stands over the water at the east end of the lake. It has a small terrace in front. It is accompanied by storied buildings on its right and left sides as well as to the rear, thus making for perfect acoustics when musical performances are given in the pavilion. It is exquisitely built, with rich carvings on the roof ridges and the eaves.

Hudie Ting (Butterfly Hall), Heyuan Garden, Yangzhou / next page

Heyuan Garden, located in Diaojia Lane in the southeast part of Yangzhou, used to be the residence of a He family. The Hudie Ting (Butterfly Hall), standing to the north of the lake, is the main building in the garden. It is a large two-storied building with a spacious terrace in front facing the lake. The upper story extends into a parallel roofed walkway to the east, and a long roofed walkway to the south. The lake in the center is thus embraced on the north, south and east sides by roofed walkways. On the upper story, access is provided by walkways all round. This is a unique example of how storied buildings in gardens can be adopted.

**Dragon wall in front of Hexu Tang (Warm and Peaceful Hall), Yuyuan
Garden** / opposite page

Yuyuan Garden is located in the northeast of the old Shanghai county now within the city
district of Shanghai. First built during the Ming Dynasty, the garden was owned by Pan
Yunduan, who was once a government official in Sichuan Province. "Yu" in Chinese means
"happy", which discloses his intention in building the garden: to make his parents happy.
Hexu Tang (Warm and Peaceful Hall) in the eastern part of the garden is square in plan, with
rocks and plantings to the fore and a lake behind. On top of the whitewashed wall in front of
the hall there are two dragons striving to procure the flame-like precious pearl between them.
Two open tracery windows are arranged symmetrically on the two sides of the door, but are
of different design. Standing beneath them are two stone lions of lively expression.

**Chuanyun Longqiang (Dragon Wall Piercing Through Clouds) in Yuyuan
Garden (Happy Garden)**

This wall, Chuanyun Longqiang (Dragon Wall Piercing Through Clouds), is to the west of
Dianchuntang Hall. The dragon on the top of the wall has an undulating shape, and so
dramatic that it seems to be flying through the clouds. There is a moon-gate entrance in
the whitewashed wall, leading through a winding roofed walkway to Wanhua Lou (Storied
Building with Thousands of Flowers).

Roof of Jianrujiajing (Roofed Walkway Leading Gradually into a Realm of Splendor), Yuyuan Garden

Jianrujiajing (Roofed Walkway Leading Gradually into a Realm of Splendor) is in the northwest part of the garden on the east side of the lake. It leads to Wanhua Lou, Yule Xie (Happy Fish Waterside Pavilion) and several other courtyards. Plants line both sides, and the design of its roof is especially noteworthy. The roof ridges are all upturned, and decorated with a wide variety of carved figures. The roof tiles are laid in rows with grooves between for drainage.

Dachang Tai (Storied Pavilion for Singing and Playing Musical Instruments), Yuyuan Garden / opposite page

Located to the south of Dianchuntang Hall, north of Hexu Tang, Dachang Tai is a storied pavilion for singing and playing musical instruments. It is exquisitely built and luxuriously decorated. The roof ridges of both the upper and lower stories curve dramatically upwards. As it is sited near the lake, it is in a way a water pavilion, which could thus not only be used for musical performances, but for enjoying the scenery in the garden as well.

Pond and rockery in front of Wanhua Lou (Storied Building with Thousands of Flowers) and perforated wall across the water, Yuyuan Garden

Located to the northeast of Liangyixuan Lounge, Wanhua Lou (Storied Building with Thousands of Flowers) faces Changbao Lou (Storied Building for Valuables) in the east. The artificial hill in front of the building is of earth, overlaid with Taihu rocks on top, and partly encircled by a whitewashed wall. Plants grow in profusion over the hill and among the rocks. The inverted images of the hill in the lake add charm to the surroundings.

Jiushi Xuan (Nine Lion Pavilion), Yuyuan Garden

Bordering on water, Jiushi Xuan (Nine Lion Pavilion) is located on the northern edge of one of the lakes. The terrace to the fore is built over the water and supported by stone piles driven into the bed of the lake. It is situated outside the southwest wall of Yule Xie (Happy Fish Waterside Pavilion), and has Huijing Lou (Storied Building for Enjoying Scenery) to its east. The lake in front contains an abundance of lotus flowers. Lying in the shade of ancient trees, it is an ideal place for enjoying the cool in summer time.

Grand rockery, Yuyuan Garden

The grand rockery hill in Yuyuan Garden is a masterpiece among the artificial hills in private gardens in the region to the south of Yangtze River, and is also a surviving example of the art of rockery making during the Ming Dynasty. Rising up to 12 meters, it is built with yellow stones from Zhejiang Province. It has range upon range of peaks, cliffs and precipices, winding paths and steps through the rocks, grottos and waterfalls, and plants growing in profusion. The small pavilion sitting on top is named Wang Jiang (Looking to the River), because in the old days, one could have an unobstructed view of boats on the Huangpu River from the top of the hill a clever means of view borrowing.

Pond in front of Huijing Lou (Storied Building for Enjoying Scenery), Yuyuan Garden

Huijing Lou (Storied Building for Enjoying Scenery) is located to the east of the lake in the central part of the garden. Rockeries line the bank, with stones projecting into the water. A zigzag bridge spans over the lake. On the west side of the building, there are also artificial hills piled with Taihu stones. The whitewashed wall has a moon-gate entrance and a number of perforated windows. These serve to connect inside and outside, thus alleviating the feeling of confinement.

A garden scene taken from the southern side of the lake in Zuibaichi Garden (Garden of the Drunken Poet)

During the Ming and Qing dynasties, private gardens prospered in the county town of Songjiang, and quite a number of these gardens were on a large scale. Yet, Zuibaichi Garden (Garden of the Drunken Poet) is the only one to have survived and to have retained its original appearance. The lake in the garden is divided into the east and west sections, with the moon-gate entrance in the picture located to the south. Looking through the doorway, one can see dark-coloured balustrades in the foreground, the lake, lotus flowers, and rockeries in the center, and the pavilion with its beams, columns and latticework windows in the distance. Further on, a whitewashed wall and dark tiles are just visible. The door opening acts as a picture frame, through which the beautiful scenery in the garden can be enjoyed.

Thatched cottage by the lake, Zuibaichi Garden / opposite lower

The thatched cottage is built across the water. It is a four-sided hall with a veranda running round it. Leaning against the balustrades, one can see water flowing under the building and fish swimming leisurely in the lake. Gigantic trees grow in front of the cottage, and bamboo behind. Interestingly shaped stones line the banks of the lake. A tablet carved with the name of the building is hung in the middle of the beam. The famous Tang poet Bai Juyi, careworn and tired of officialdom, had a house built by the lake in his old residence in Luoyang. There, he drank and composed poems every day, and took pleasure in getting drunk. The garden takes its name from this story of Bai Juyi.

Biwu Xuan (Hall of Emerald Green Phoenix Trees) and Biguang Ting (Pavilion in Emerald Green Light) in Qiuxiapu Garden (Orchard in Autumn Evening Glow)

Qiuxiapu Garden (Orchard in Autumn Evening Glow), enclosed within whitewashed walls and black gates, is located on East Street in the county town of Jiading. It was built in Ming times as a private garden attached to the residence of the court minister Gong Hong. Biwu Xuan (Hall of Emerald Green Phoenix Trees) to the north of the lake is the main building in the garden. A spacious terrace is built in front of it on the bank of the lake. The building is simple and unadorned. Biguang Ting (Pavilion in Emerald Green Light) is built into the water to the southwest of the hall. It is actually a waterside pavilion open on three sides, and an ideal place to enjoy the moon in autumn.

Zhou'erbuyou Xuan (Boat-not-for-Rowing Hall), Qiuxiapu Garden

Zhou'erbuyou Xuan (Boat-not-for-Rowing Hall) is a land boat standing by the side of Conggui Xuan (Sweet Osmanthus Hall). The head of the "boat" borders on the lake facing east, and the body of the "boat" is actually a small hall. On autumn days, the air is full of the fragrance of sweet osmanthus, which adds greatly to the charm of the place. It is an ideal spot for drinking tea, playing chess, reading, enjoying the scenery and entertaining friends.

East corner of the lake in Qiuxiapu Garden

The stone bridge in the picture leads to Pingshan Hall on the eastern side of the lake. The bridge is only wide enough for one person to pass at a time. The top of the balusters at the two ends of the bridge are carved into the shape of the lotus flower, while the ones in the middle are lion-shaped. A gigantic ancient tree stands in front of Pingshan Hall, its leaves making whispering sounds when wind passes through. Fish swim about leisurely in the lake, recalling the Taoist philosophy of "knowing the happiness of the fish".

Winding dyke, Qiyuan Garden (Charming Garden), Haiyan / opposite upper

The winding dyke lying low on the water conveys the impression of a belt floating on the lake. It is a rare example in a private garden of innovative water treatment to achieve spatial effects. Old trees lining the lake provide cool shade even on hot summer days. After crossing the winding dyke, one will come to an arched bridge, which leads to other scenic spots.

Yanhua Bridge, Qiyuan Garden, Haiyan / opposite lower

The arched Yanhua Bridge stands at the north end of the long dyke. It is of simple design, and conveys the impression of age. The top of the balusters is decorated with expressive stone lions . Old trees cast deep shadows over the bridge, which is surrounded by scenery that is delightful all year round.

Flowery hall, Qiyuan Garden, Haiyan

The flowery hall is called Tanying Xuan (Hall with Reflection in the Pool). It has large windows on four sides to facilitate enjoyment of the surrounding scenery. The roof ridges turn gracefully upwards. Embedded as the hall is in surroundings beautified by flowing water and a rustic bridge, luxuriant trees and flowers and bizarrely shaped rocks, the impression one has as one listens to the song of birds and the rustling of leaves is that of being in a wild country, far away from the bustle of city life.

Scenery in the central part of Keyuan Garden, Dongguan

The path in the picture paved with reddish stones bears the name of Huazhijing (Flower Passage) because it used to be lined with flowers on both sides and a trellis of wistaria. On the right side of the path is a terrace for orchids. The building with a hip-and-gable roof in the distance is the residence of the owner of the garden. It is splendid in appearance, and its interior furnishing refined.

Kelou Storied Building, Keyuan Garden, Dongguan / opposite page

Built during the Xianfeng reign (1851-1861) of the Qing Dynasty, Keyuan Garden is a typical example of a garden surrounded by a group of storied buildings. Kelou, a four-storied tower measuring 16 meters in height, is the main building in the garden. The first story is called Ke Xuan (Ke Hall), whereas the topmost story has been given the name of Yaoshan Ge (Invitation to Mountains Pavilion). It is the tallest building in the garden, and, in the past, was the tallest in Dongwan County. The group of buildings encircling the garden vary in height as well as in spacing, and winding roofed walkways are used to connect the different parts. The scenery in the garden can thus be viewed from many different angles. Of all the Chinese classical gardens, this is the only one that has such a unique layout.

Winding Roofed Walkway in Yuyinshanfang (Mounain Villa with Ancestral Blessings), Panyu

Yuyinshanfang (Mountain Villa with Ancestral Blessings) was built during the Tongzhi reign (1862-1874) of the Qing Dynasty. It is an area of only 2,000 square meters, but has been given a compact layout of artificial hills and a lake, as well as halls, pavilions, roofed walkways and bridges. The buildings are arranged round the covered walkway, which is a particular characteristic of gardens in the Guangdong area. The winding roofed walkway in the picture is connected with Linglong Shuixie (Exquisite Waterside Pavilion). Small in scale and modest in form and colour, it gives the impression of forming a harmonious whole with the waterside pavilion. Rare flowers and trees line the walkway on both sides, and potted miniature landscapes serve as decoration. The garden is richly planted with sweet osmanthus, bamboo, cypresses and orchids, and interestingly shaped rocks are dotted about.

Interior view of Linglong Shuixie (Exquisite Waterside Pavilion), Yuyinshanfang, Panyu

Linglong Shuixie (Exquisite Waterside Pavilion) is octagonal in plan and surrounded by water. Long windows with pretty traceries are installed on all sides of the pavilion. The interior furnishing is refined and tasteful, and harmonizes in colour with the window frames. This is the place where the master of the garden enjoyed the scenery and composed poems.

Minor lodge by the side of pool in Yuyinshanfang, Panyu

The lodge is on the east side of the lotus pond. It has three bays widthwise, the third actually being a passageway. The house has been given openwork screens in ice-crack patterns and decorative windows painted in gold. It is a splendid and elegant building, and in front of the lodge, there is a terrace with balustrades.

Zhengrong Jiashan (Towering Rockery Hill) viewed from the doorway of the winding roofed walkway, Yuyinshanfang, Panyu

The door at the end of the roofed walkway has full-length openwork screen on both sides, which divides up the space without obstructing the view. A couplet is carved on the bamboo plates hung on both sides of the doorway. After passing through the doorway, one is faced by the huge, grand-looking Zhengrong Jiashan (Towering Rockery Hill). Bamboos are planted by its side. There is a small path leading through the rockery, so narrow that one can only just squeeze through. This rockery arrangement is unique, and quite different to that employed in Suzhou, Yangzhou, or other cities in the Yangtze River region.

Stained glass windowpanes in Shenliu Tang (Hall in the Depth of Willows), Yuyinshanfang, Panyu

These exquisite and hexagonal-patterned windows with their blue and white panes and strikingly red floral centrepiece are to be found in a side room in Shenliu Tang (Hall in the Depth of Willows). It is the main building in the garden, and its architecture is typical of the Guangdong area. The refined interior decoration harmonizes well with the magnificent exterior.

Glossary

"One lake and three islands"
A typical mode in Chinese traditional garden building. The creation of miniature mountains and stretches of water by simulating natural landscape is the basic method adopted for classical Chinese gardens. The layout pattern of building "hills", or islands, in lakes is a typical characteristic in the landscape architecture of gardens.

nine-dragon wall
In the Ming and Qing dynasties, large screen walls built of glazed bricks and tiles with reliefs of nine dragons.

earth hill
One kind of miniature mountain in Chinese gardens, piled up entirely with earth, on which trees are planted to give the impression of profusely wooded mountains.

taihu stone
The most important type of stone used for garden building. Being a kind of lime rock, they are divided into the northern and the southern type, and can be found in water or in mountains. Those found in the Taihu Lake are the most famous, hence "Taihu" becomes a general name for such stones.

shuifa
Artificial fountain.

shui lang
One kind of roofed walkway built on the waterside or over the surface of the water.

tai
High platform or terrace built in ancient times for emperors to offer sacrifices to Heaven. The emperor was able to look far into the distance from the top of the platform, and so it became a symbol for the mountains. In later ages, it gradually became a kind of structure in gardens for entertainment purposes.

projecting rock
A kind of scenic creation in gardens. Rocks are built in such a way that they project horizontally over the surface of the water. One can sit fishing on the rocks while water will keep flowing underneath. Hence, they are also called "fishing rocks".

qu lang
Curved roofed walkway, one kind of roofed walkway in gardens. One is led on by such walkways, and the scenes presented before one vary as one moves along.

chi
Pond, a kind of water landscape in gardens. A pond is generally small, and the water in it is still. It is often found in gardens of comparatively small scope, or in scenic areas in large gardens.

Buddhist pagoda
Originated in India, it is a kind of storied structure built of wood, brick or stone to store Buddhist relics or scripts. It is often square or octagonal in plan, and its stories are generally in odd numbers.

yong dao
Corridor connecting buildings or pavilions.

fang
Subsidiary small square beam.

pashan lang
Roofed walkway ascending a hill, one kind of roofed walkway in gardens. It is built on undulating hill slopes to connect buildings on different

elevations. There are steps on the walkway, and its roof is either sloped or has a number of drops.

pavilion
A kind of building structure in gardens, which can be round, square, or polygonal in plan.

you
In ancient China, an enclosure within which birds and animals were kept for the hunting and entertainment requirements of emperors and aristocrats.

quan
Spring, a kind of water landscape in gardens, built according to natural conditions.

fei ge
Flying corridor, elevated corridor constructed to connect buildings.

borrowed view
One of the traditional methods used in Chinese garden architecture, by which the sight presented to the visitor is enriched by incorporating into the view beautiful scenes in or out of the garden.

gong guan
In ancient China, a kind of building structure in you for the rest or recreation of emperors.

island
Small piece of land surrounded by water in ponds or lakes. It is a kind of water landscape in gardens. By "one lake and three islands", it means the building of islands in waters.

xuan
A kind of open hall often seen in gardens, generally built at minor scenic spots.

hui lang
Winding roofed walkway, one kind of roofed walkway in gardens, used to enclose courtyards.

courtyard
An important feature in Chinese garden architecture. The buildings are encircled by winding roofed walkways or walls so as to form spatial segments or scenic areas. The aim of such a measure is to create small gardens within a large garden or scenic spots within the general scope of natural scenery.

glazed tile
The tiles are mostly green and yellow in colour, but can also be in black, blue or other colors. They are generally used for palace and temple buildings.

bian e
Horizontal inscribed tablet hung in halls or pavilions.

imperial passage
Stone strip in the center of the flight of steps leading up the podium to the front of the palace hall. It is generally decorated with relief carvings of dragon, phoenix and cloud patterns, and flanked on both sides with steps. It is not actually to walk on, but the emperor, seated in his sedan chair, would pass over this stone strip when going up the podium to the palace hall.

baluster column
Stanchions between railing panels on balustrades.

garden building
To plan and design an enclosed area according to certain functional requirements and artistic conceptions, and based on such natural phenomena as mountains, hills, water, and plants, and to put up buildings in accordance with the general motif, so that a comprehensive creation with social, environmental and aesthetic values is achieved to satisfy man's material and spiritual needs.

Lamaist dagoba
It is often described as a pagoda in the shape of an upside-down bowl. The main structure is hemispherical in shape, standing on a setback podium. On top of the main structure is the tee, which consists of four sections, the base, the post, the umbrella-shaped cover and the top.

wall
Structure with no coverage on top, for spatial partition only, but not for shelter from the elements.

dike
A bank built on watersides or across water, generally used for large expanses of water, in order to keep water at bay, to control the water level, to divide water surface, to create scenic spots, or to serve as the basis for building roads.

scenic spot
A basic unit in gardens. All natural and man-made scenes that have aesthetic values can be defined as a scenic spot. A scenic area consists of several scenic spots, and a garden comprises a number of scenic areas.

lake
A kind of water landscape in gardens, generally referring to large areas of water surface. It can include natural lakes, such as the West Lake in Hangzhou and Xuanwu Lake in Nanjing, or lakes in imperial gardens, such as Beihai Lake in the center of Beijing and Kunming Lake in the Summer Palace.

beamless hall
Structures consisting entirely of vaults built with bricks or stones. The external appearance of such buildings looks like the ancient wooden structures, although actually built of bricks or stones.

archway
A gateway-like structure for memorial purposes, but can also serve as spatial partition; generally built of wood, brick, stone, or glazed bricks.

garden
See "garden building".

mei
Lintel, horizontal piece of timber over a door.

you lang
Connective roofed walkway, one kind of roofed walkway in gardens, used for joining separate, independent buildings in a cluster of buildings, and for linking or segmenting outdoor spaces.

partition wall
Vertical members for separating indoor spaces according to requirements. Being non-loadbearing,

it can be more flexibly arranged and fixed directly on the floor.

xie
Terraced pavilion, one of the principal forms of buildings in gardens, originally meaning buildings put up on podiums. Such buildings are generally constructed on watersides, so are also called "water pavilions".

perforated window
Also known as flowery window. Such windows, generally made of bricks in various openwork patterns, are set in walls for ornamental purpose.

white marble
A kind of marble, white in color and high in density, and thus an excellent building material.

Mongolian yurt
Residence of Mongolian nomads. The circular wall of the tent is built of timber strips arranged net-like, and a wooden door frame put up in the wall. The umbrella-shaped roof is built of wooden rafters, and covered with felt rugs tightened by ropes. In the middle of the roof there is a skylight. The yurt can be easily dismantled and transferred from place to place.

ge
A form of building often found in gardens. Its location and function are similar to those of multi-storied buildings, but it is usually smaller in size. It is generally built on flat land, but occasionally against hillsides. It is sometimes, also erected on watersides.

ge dao
Two-storied roofed corridor closed on both sides, a kind of roofed walkway in gardens, used to connect separate, independent palace buildings.

lou
Multi-storied building in gardens used for enjoying scenery in the distance, or for relaxation and recreation.

fu dao
Elevated corridor connecting buildings or pavilions.

bridge

Chinese garden architecture is characterized by the beauty of mountains and water. Bridges in gardens are not only used to connect passages, but are also used to divide expanses of water to add variation. Such bridges are generally beautifully and gracefully shaped, and so become a scenic spot in themselves.

winged eave

A general term for the corner of the roof. It is so called because the tip of the roof corner is upturned like the wings of a bird.

dian jing

Highlighting scenic spots. At important scenic spots in gardens, measures are often taken to augment their remarkableness. The buildings there are generally given names appertaining to the environs, or inscribed with poems and couplets describing the essence of the scenery, thus adding the touch that enhances the aesthetic effect of the spot.

zhai

A form of building in gardens, built at deep and quiet places and used for studies or studios. There is no set form for such buildings, but they are generally enclosed and secluded.

que

In ancient China, structures marking the entrance to a building complex. They are generally built in pairs, and stand on the two sides of a road. Such structures can often be found in front of citadels, palaces, mansions, ancestral temples and mausoleums.

li gong

Imperial travelling resort, palace buildings for residence or entertainment of emperors built outside the capital city.

luo cheng

Small fortresses built outside the city wall as a safeguard.

Suzhou-styled coloured paintings

Coloured paintings generally used in gardens or for important buildings and large mansions. The subjects of such paintings are mostly flowers, birds, fish, figures, and landscapes.

railing panel

Stone panel on balustrades between banisters.

terrace

Roofless open platform on top of buildings.

rockery hill

Miniature mountains piled up with rocks and stones to look like natural mountains, used to decorate gardens, and sometimes placed by the side of buildings.

lin you

The enclosure for hunting and entertainment of Emperor Wenwang of the Zhou Dynasty in particular. Woodcutters and huntsmen were allowed to enter the enclosure to cut faggot and to capture small animals such as pheasants and rabbits.

Chronology of Major Events
in the History of Chinese Architecture

Christian era	Chinese Dynastic Years	Events or Achievements
The Neolithic Age		
ca. 4800 BC		Sites of ganlan buildings (pile-supported structures with wooden floor above the ground) of Hemudu Culture were unearthed in the northeast of Hemudu Village in Yuyao County, Zhejiang province.
ca. 4500 BC		Sites of Various kinds of primitive houses of Yangshao Culture, including a big house square in plan were unearthed in Banpo Village near Xi'an, Shaanxi province.
2310~2378 BC		A sacrificial altar of Liangzhu Culture was unearthed at Yaoshan in Yuhang County, Zhejiang province.
ca. 3000 BC		Temple of Goddess of Hongshan Culture was discovered at Niuheliang in Lingyuan County, Liaoning province.
The Shang Dynasty		
1900~1500 BC		An Early Shang site of a high-terrace palatial complex was unearthed at Erlitou Village in Yanshi County, Henan province.
17th~11th c. BC		Rectangular houses with rammed earth foundations and walls were unearthed in present Zhengzhou, Henan province.
1384 BC	15th year, Pangeng	Capital of the Shang was moved to Yin where the Late Shang capital was constructed, which was unearthed and referred to as the Yin Ruins at Xiaotun Village in Anyang, Henan province.
The Western Zhou Dynasty		
1095 BC	10th year, Chengwang	An ancestral temple of the Zhou Court was unearthed at Fengchu Village in Qishan County, Shaanxi province.
The Spring and Autumn Period		
475 BC	45th year, Jingwang	Rules for capital planning of the Zhou Court were recorded in the Survey on Construction Work collected in the Ritual of Zhou, in which it was regulated that the Ancestral Temple was to be located to the left of the palace, and the Altar of Land and Grain, to its right.
The Warring States Period		
350~207 BC		Site of Xianyang Palace of the Qin State, a high-terrace building complex, was unearthed at Xianyang, Shaanxi province.
The Qin Dynasty		
221 BC	26th year, Shi Huang Di	The Qin conquered the six states and built palaces in styles to imitate those of the conquered states on the northern sloping fields of Xianyang. An army of 300,000 men, led by Meng Tian, was sent to drive out the northern nomadic Hun invasions and to build the Great Wall from Lintao (in present-day Gansu province) in the west to Liaodong (the east of present-day Liaoning province) in the east. Capital Xianyang was constructed and extended.
221~210 BC	26th~37th years, Shi Huang Di	Construction of Shi Huang Di's mausoleum started in Lintong, Shaanxi province.
212 BC	35th year, Shi Huang Di	Construction of the Epang (or Efanggong) Palace began on the south bank of the Wei River, Xianyang.
The Western Han Dynasty		
200 BC	7th year, Gaozu	Palatial city in Chang'an (present-day Xi'an) was under construction and Chang Le Palace (Palace of Everlasting Happiness) was erected.
199 BC	8th year, Gaozu	Construction of Wei Yang palace started. The Palace was completed in the next year.
140~87 BC	Reign period of Wudi	Construction of Maoling Tomb (the Mausoleum of Emperor Wudi) started in Xingping County, Shaanxi province.
138 BC	4th year, Jianyuan, Wudi	Shang Lin Garden of the Qin was extended in a vast area of 300 li across with 70 detached palaces included.
127 BC	2nd year, Yuanshuo, Wudi	The Great Wall with watchtowers, passes and beacon towers was reconstructed. Later on, the Great wall underwent five large-scale reconstruction works.

Christian era	Chinese Dynastic Years	Events or Achievements
104 BC	1st year, Taichu, Wudi	Jian Zhang Palace was built in the western outskirts of Chang'an City.
101 BC	4th year, Taichu, Wudi	Ming Guang Palace was built in the City of Chang'an.
32 BC	1st year, Jianshi, Chengdi	Altars for offering sacrifices to God of Heaven and God of Earth were erected in the southern and northern suburbs of Chang'an respectively. Thereafter the locations of the Altar of Heaven and the Altar of Earth in the planning of the capital city were so established as a rule.
4 AD	4th year, Yuanshi, Pingdi	Mingtang, Biyong (halls for handling state affairs and promulgating politics as well as schooling) and Lingtai (Terrace of Spirit) were erected inside and outside Chang'an.
The Xin Dynasty		
20 AD	1st year, Dihuang, Wang Mang	More than ten palaces, including Jian Zhang Palace, were demolished. The disassembled materials were used to build eleven buildings in the southern suburbs of Chang'an, known as the Nine Temples of Wang Mang historically.
The Eastern Han Dynasty		
68 AD	11th year, Yongping, Mingdi	Baima Si (the Temple of White Horse) was erected in Luoyang.
Period of the Three Kingdoms		
220 AD	1st year, Huangchu, Wendi of the Wei	Cao Pi founded the Kingdom of Wei with its capital moved from Yecheng to Luoyang.
221 AD	1st year, Zhangwu, the Shu Han	Liu Bei founded the Kingdom of Shu Han, making Chengdu (in present-day Sichuan province) its capital.
229 AD	8th year, Huangwu, the Wu	Sun Quan moved the capital of the Kingdom of Wu from Wuchang to Jianye (present-day Nanjing). The capital city with the palace were then constructed.
235 AD	3rd year, Qinglong, Mingdi of the Wei	The Palace of Luoyang of the Wei Court was built at Luoyang.
237 AD	1st year, Jingchu, Mingdi of the Wei	The Garden of Fragrant Forest (Fang Lin Yuan) was completed and the Hill of Jingyang was piled up in Luoyang
The Jin Dynasty		
ca. 300 AD	ca. 1st year, Yongkang, Huidi	Shi Chong built a garden at the Golden Ravine in the northeastern outskirts of Luoyang, known as the Garden of Golden Ravine.
332 AD	7th year, Xianhe, Chengdi	The Palace of Jiankang was built in Jiankang (present-day Nanjing).
347 AD	3rd year, Yonghe, Mudi	An imperial garden called Hualin Garden was built at the southern bank of Xuanwu Lake in Jiankang. About a hundred years later, the Song of the Southern Dynasties built another garden called the Pleasure Garden to the east of Hualin Garden.
353~366 AD		Mogao Grottoes at Dunhuang, in present-day Gansu province, were first dug out.
400 AD	4th year, Long'an, Andi	Buddhist Monk Huichi built the Temple of Samantabhadra (present-day the Wannian Temple) at Mount Emei in Sichuan.
413 AD	9th year, Yixi, Andi	Helianbobo built Tongwancheng, capital city of the Great Xia Dynasty (in presentday Inner Mongolia).
The Northern and Southern Dynasties		
452~464 AD	Wenchengdi, Northern Wei	Yungang Grottoes at Datong, Shanxi, were first hollowed out.
494~495 AD	18th~19th years, Taihe, Northern Wei	Longmen Grottoes at Luoyang, Henan, were first hollowed out.
513 AD	2nd year, Yanchang, Northern Wei	Grottoes of Bingling Temple, a Buddhist cave temple in Gansu, was built.
516 AD	1st year, Xiping, Northern Wei	Wooden Pagoda of the Temple of Everlasting Tranquillity (Yongning Temple) was erected up in Luoyang.
523 AD	4th year, Zhengguang, Northern Wei	Brick Pagoda of the Songyue Temple at Dengfeng in Henan was built.
The Sui Dynasty		
582	2nd year, Kaihuang, Wendi	Yuwen Kai was appointed to design and construct the capital city Daxing (present-day Xi'an), which was renamed as Chang'an in the Tang Dynasty.
586	6th year, Kaihuang, Wendi	Construction of the Longzang Buddhist Temple at Zhengding, Hebei, started. The temple was renamed as the Longxing Temple in the reign period of Emperor Kangxi of the Qing Dynasty.
595	15th year, Kaihuang, Wendi	Palace of Benevolence and Longevity (Ren Shou Gong) was built in Daxing, capital of the Sui Dynasty.
607	3rd year, Daye, Yangdi	One million men were sent to repair and restore the Great Wall.
611	7th year, Daye, Yangdi	The Four-Gate Pagoda, a single-storeyed pagoda, of Shentong Temple in Licheng, Shandong, was built.

Christian era	Chinese Dynastic Years	Events or Achievements
The Tang Dynasty		
618~916		Double-storeyed single-sealed dwelling houses came into being, while multi-storeyed buildings became on the wane.
627~648	Period of Zhenguan, Taizong	Mount Hua in Shaanxi, one of the Five Sacred Mountains in ancient China, was granted as the Golden Heavenly King, where the Temple of Western Sacred Mountain was built.
630	4th year, Zhenguan, Taizong	Orders were given to erect Confucian Temples in the schools of prefectures and counties all over the country.
636	10th year, Zhenguan, Taizong	Construction of Zhaoling Tomb (the Mausoleum of Emperor Taizong) began in Liquan County, Shaanxi.
651	2nd year, Yonghui,Gaozong	Taziks (the Arabian Empire) sent envoys to the Tang Court. Since then, the Islamic architecture came into being in China.
7th century		Huaisheng Si (literally, the Mosque in Memory of the Saint) was first built in Guangzhou, Guangdong.
652	3rd year, Yonghui,Gaozong	The Great Wild Goose Pagoda of Cien Temple in Chang'an (present-day Xi'an) was built.
669	2nd year, Zongzhang,	The Pagoda of Xuanzang was built in Xingjiao Temple in Chang'an.
681	1st year, Kaiyao, Gaozong	The Pagoda of Xiangji Temple in Chang'an was built.
683	1st year, Hongdao, Gaozong	Construction of Qianling Tomb (the Mausoleum of Emperor Gaozong) began in Qianxian County, Shaanxi.
707~709	1st~3rd years, Jinglong,Zhongzong	The Small Wild Goose Pagoda of Jianfu Temple in Chang'an was built.
714	2nd year, Kaiyuan,Xuanzong	Construction of Xingqing Palace in Chang'an started.
722	10th year, Kaiyuan, Xuanzong	The Tianchang Taoist Temple in Youzhou (present-day Beijing) was first built. The Temple was renamed as Baiyun Guan, or the Temple of White Clouds, in the early Ming Dynasty.
724	12th year, Kaiyuan, Xuanzong	Jianfu Palace at the foot of Qingcheng Mountain in Sichuan was first built.
725	13th year, Kaiyuan, Xuanzong	The Huaqing Pool with a detached palace was built at Lishan in Lintong County, Shaanxi. The Qujiang Pool with a recreation garden was built in Chang'an.
782	3rd year, Jianzhong, Dezong	The Main Hall of Nanchan Temple in Mount Wutai, Shanxi, was built.
857	11th year, Dazhong, Xuanzong	The Eastern Hall of Foguang Temple in Mount Wutai, Shanxi, was built.
The Five Dynasties		
956	3rd year, Xiande,Shizong, Late Zhou	The Later Zhou made Kaifeng the capital, and then, extended it on the basis of the capital of the Later Liang and Later Jin. Thereafter, Kaifeng was further developed especially when it was made capital of the Northern Song Dynasty.
959	6th year, Xiande,Shizong, Late Zhou	The Pagoda of Yunyan Temple at Suzhou, Jiangsu, was built.
The Northern Song and Liao (Khitan)Dynasties		
960~1279		Style and form of local dwelling houses were gradually finalized with less difference from those of the Qing period.
964	2nd year, Qiande,Taizu, the Song	The Temple of Central Sacred Mountain at Songshan, Henan, was renovated.
971	4th year, Kaibao,Taizu, the Song	The Pavilion of Buddha Fragrance (Foxiang Ge) at Longxing Temple in Zhengding, Hebei, was first built with a 24-metre-high bronze statue of Guanyin (Goddess of Mercy, or Avalokitesvara) housed in.
977	2nd year, Taipingxingguo,Taizong, the Song	The Longhua Pagoda was erected in Shanghai.
984	2nd year, Tonghe,Shengzong, the Liao	The Guanyin Pavilion and the Entrance Hall of Dule Temple at Jixian County in presentday Tianjin were built.
996	14th year, Tonghe,Shengzong, the Liao	Libai Si of Niujie, or the Mosque of Ox Street, in Beijing was first built.
1009	2nd year, Dazhongxiangfu,Zhenzong, the Song	Tiankuang Dian (literally, the Hall of Godsend) of Dai Miao (Temple of Eastern Sacred Mountain) was built on the foot of Mount Tai, Shandong. Temple of Princess Aurora was built on the top of Mount Tai.
1009	2nd year, Dazhongxiangfu,Zhenzong, the Song	The Ashab Mosque at Quanzhou, Fujian, was first built.

Christian era	Chinese Dynastic Years	Events or Achievements
1038	7th year, Chongxi,Xingzong, the Liao	The Bhagavat Storage Hall (Bojia Jiaozang Dian) of the Lower Huayan Temple in Datong, Shanxi, was built.
1052	4th year, Huangyou,Renzong, the Song	The Hall of Sakyamuni (Moni Dian) of Longxing Temple in Zhengding, Hebei, was built.
1056	2nd year, Qingning,Daozong, the Liao	The Pagoda of Sakyamuni, or the Wooden Pagoda, of Fogong Temple at Yingxian, Shanxi, was erected.
1100	3rd year, Yuanfu,Zhezong, the Song	Li Jie finalized the book Building Standard, or treatise On Architectural Methods, which was promulgated by the Song Court in 1103 as building codes for design and construction works.
1102	1st year, Chongning,Huizong, the Song	The Shengmu Hall, or the Hall of Sacred Mother, of Jin Ci, a memorial temple of Jin, in Taiyuan, Shanxi, was restored.
1115	5th year, Zhenghe,Huizong, the Song	It is recorded that there were more than ten thousand workers everyday forced to build Mingtang for the emperor in Kaifeng.
1125	7th year, Xuanhe,Huizong, the Song	The Chuzu Nunnery, or the Hall of Patriarch, of Shaolin Temple in Dengfeng, Henan, was built.
12th century		The Minaret of Light was built in Huaisheng Si, or the Mosque in Memory of the Saint, in Guangzhou, Guangdong.

The Southern Song and Jin (Jurchen)Dynasties

12th century		Han Tuozhou built his personal garden, called the Southern Garden, in Lin'an (present-day Hangzhou). Han Shizong built his personal garden, called Meigang Garden (literally, the Garden of Plum Blossom Ridge), in Lin'an.
1138	8th year, Shaoxing,Gaozong, the Song	The Song Court moved to Lin'an where the temporary palace was arranged. Lin'an was then decided upon as the temporary capital and was extended.
1150	2nd year, Tiande,Qingdi, the Jin	Wanyan Liang, emperor of the Jurchen (Jin), renamed Youzhou (present-day Beijing) as the Middle Capital of the Jurchen, and assigned Zhang Hao and Kong Yanzhou to the construction of the Middle Capital.
1163	3rd year, Dading,Shizong, the Jin	The Confucian Temple with its main hall, Dacheng Dian, at Pingyao, Shanxi, was built.
1240	12th year, Taizong of the Mongols	The Palace of Perpetual Happiness, or Yongle Gong, was built at Yongle Town in Yongji County, Shanxi. It is a Taoist temple in memory of Lu Dongbin, one of the Eight Taoist Immortals, and it was said that Yongle Town was Lu Dongbin's birthplace.
1267	4th year, Zhiyuan,Shizu of the Mongols	The Mongol Emperor Kublai Khan moved the capital to Youzhou (present-day Beijing), and renamed it as Dadu, or the Great Capital. Liu Bingzhong was appointed to plan and construct the Great Capital.
1269	6th year, ZhiyuanShizu of the Mongols	The Imperial College (the highest educational administration) was established in Dadu (the Great Capital).
1271	8th year, Zhiyuan,Shizu of the Yuan	In Miaoying Temple, a Lamasery in Beijing, the White Dagoba, which is a pagoda in Lamaist style, was erected. It is the earliest dagoba preserved intact in China.
1275	1st year, Deyou,Gongdi, the Song	Tomb of Puhading, sixteenth generation descendent of Mohammed, was built in Yangzhou, Jiangsu. Xianhe Si (literally, the Mosque of White Crane) was erected in Yangzhou.

The Yuan Dynasty

13th century	Early Yuan Period	The Southern Temple of Saga in Saga County, Tibet, was built.
13th century	Early Yuan Period	The Hill of Longevity and the Imperial Lake were constructed in Dadu (the Great Capital) as the Imperial Garden of the Yuan Court. The Hill of Longevity was constructed on the Jade Flower Islet (or Qionghua Island) of the Jin, which is in Beihai Park of today's Beijing.
1302	6th year, Dade, Chengzong	The Confucian Temple in Dadu (present-day Beijing) was built.
1309	2nd year, Zhida, Wuzong	The Ashab Mosque at Quanzhou, Fujian, was renovated.
1323	3rd year, Zhizhi, Yingzong	Islamic Holy Tombs of Quanzhou, Fujian, were renovated.
1342	2nd year, Zhizheng, Shundi	Tian Ru, a Buddhist abbot, built the Shizi Lin (Garden of Lion Grove) in Suzhou.
1350	10th year, Zhizheng, Shundi	Huaisheng Si, or the Mosque in Memory of the Saint, in Guangzhou was renovated.
1356	16th year, Zhizheng, Shundi	The Mosque of Dongsi in Beijing was first built. It was renovated in 1447.
1363	23rd year, Zhizheng, Shundi	Mausoleum of Tuheluk Timur at Huocheng near Gulja (Yining), Xinjiang, was built.

The Ming Dynasty

1368	1st year, Hongwu,Taizu	The Ming Court began to construct its imperial palace in Nanjing

Christian era	Chinese Dynastic Years	Events or Achievements
1373	6th year, Hongwu, Taizu	Construction of the Capital City of Nanjing as well as the imperial palace was completed. General Xu Da was appointed to garrison the northern frontiers. Based on Hua Yunlong's proposal, the Great Wall was first rebuilt. It was renovated and extended several times in the Ming period. Temple for Offering Sacrifices to Emperors of the Past Dynasties was built on the southern slope of Qintian Hill in Nanjing.
1376~1383	9th~15th year, Hongwu, Tai	The Main Hall of Linggu Temple, a vaulted beamless building, in Nanjing was built.
1381	14th year, Hongwu, Taizu	Construction of Xiaoling Tomb (the Mausoleum of Emperor Taizu) started in Nanjing. The Tomb was completed in 1405.
1407	5th year, Yongle, Chengzu	Construction of the Forbidden City in Beijing began.
1409	7th year, Yongle, Chengzu	Construction of Changling Tomb (the Mausoleum of Emperor Yongle) began in Changping County, Beijing.
1413	11th year, Yongle, Chengzu	An imperial order was given to build Taoist building complexes in Wudang Mountain, Hubei. It took 11 years to build up 8 palaces, 2 temples, 36 nunneries and 72 cliff temples.
1420	18th year, Yongle, Chengzu	City of Beijing with the Imperial City and Forbidden City included was completed. Capital of the Ming moved to Beijing. In Beijing, the Altar of Heaven, the Altar of Earth, the Imperial Ancestral Temple and the Altar of Agriculture were built.
1421	19th year, Yongle, Chengzu	The Three Great Halls of the Forbidden City were destroyed by fire. The Altar of Land and Grain in Beijing was built.
1436	1st year, Zhengtong, Yingzong	The Three Great Halls of the Forbidden City were rebuilt.
1442	7th year, Zhengtong,Yingzong	Libai Si of Niujie, or the Mosque of Ox Street, in Beijing was renovated. The Mosque was thoroughly restored and extended in 1696.
1444	9th year, Zhengtong,Yingzong	Zhihua Temple in Beijing was built.
1447	12th year, Zhengtong,Yingzong	Tashilhunpo Monastery was built in Xigaze, Tibet.
1473	9th year, Chenghua,Xianzong	Diamond Throne Pagodas (Vajrasana Pagoda, which is a five-pagoda cluster) as well as the Temple of True Awakening where the Pagodas housed were built in Beijing.
1483~1487	19th~23rd year,Chenghua, Xianzong,	The layout of Confucian Temple in Qufu, Shandong, was completed in today's range and appearance.
1506~1521	Reign Period of Zhengde, Wuzong	Jichang Garden in Wuxi, Jiangsu, was built. It was famous for its "Eight-Scaled Ravine".
1509	4th year, Zhengde, Wuzong	Wang Xianchen, a censor of the Court, dismissed from office and returned to his home town Suzhou, where he built a garden and named it "Zhuozheng Yuan" (the Humble Administrator's Garden).
1519	14th year, Zhengde, Wuzong	The Palace of Heavenly Purity and Palace of Earthly Tranquillity in the Forbidden City of Beijing, were rebuilt.
1522~1566	Reign Period of Jiajing, Shizong	Liu Yuan, or the Lingering Garden, in Suzhou was first built. It was restored in the Qing Dynasty.
1530	9th year, Jiajing, Shizong	Altar of Earth, Altar of the Sun and Altar of the Moon were constructed in the outskirts of Beijing. A series of sacrifices to Heaven, Earth, the Sun and the Moon in the four outskirts of the capital city were restored. Altar of Agriculture was rebuilt.
1531	10th year, Jiajing, Shizong	Temple for Offering Sacrifices to Emperors of the Past Dynasties was built in Beijing.
1534	13th year, Jiajing, Shizong	The Altar of Heaven and Earth in Beijing was turned into the Altar of Heaven, or the Temple of Heaven.
1537	16th year, Jiajing, Shizong	The Hall of Mental Cultivation in the Forbidden City in Beijing was newly built.
1540	19th year, Jiajing, Shizong	The Stone Pailou of the Ming Tombs in Changping, Beijing, was erected.
1545	24th year, Jiajing, Shizong	The Imperial Ancestral Temple in Beijing was rebuilt. The Main Hall of the Temple of Heaven in Beijing was rebuilt. The hall which had been rectangular in plan was changed into a triple-eaved circular building, and renamed as the Hall of Prayer for Good Harvest.
1559	38th year, Jiajing, Shizong	Being a private garden in Shanghai, Yu Yuan was built by Pan Yunduan, a retired official. The rockery there was piled up by Zhang Nanyang, a famous rockery craftsman at that time.
1568	2nd year, Longqing, Muzong	General Qi Jiguang was appointed to garrison Jizhou near Beijing. Hence the Great Wall was restored and extended, and many more beacon towers and passes were built along the Great Wall.
1573~1619	Years of Wanli, Shenzong	Mi Wanzhong built his personal garden Shao Yuan in Beijing, which was famous for its four rarities: hill, water, flowers and rocks.

Christian era	Chinese Dynastic Years	Events or Achievements
1583	11th year, Wanli, Shenzong	Construction of Dingling Tomb (the Mausoleum of Emperor Wanli) in Changping, Beijing, started.
1583	26th year, Wanli, Shenzong	The Later Jin built Xingjingling Tombs (Tombs of Imperial Ancestors of the Qing) in Xinbin, Liaoning. The Tombs were renamed as Yongling Tombs in 1659.
1615	48th year, Wanli, Shenzong	The Three Great Halls of the Forbidden City in Beijing were rebuilt.
1629	2nd year, Chongzhen, Sizong	The Later Jin built Fuling Tomb (Tomb of Nurhachi, Emperor Taizu of the Qing) in Shenyang, Liaoning.
1634	7th year, Chongzhen, Sizong	Yuan ye, a treatise on Chinese gardens written by Ji Cheng, was published.
1640	13th year, Chongzhen, Sizong	The Qing Court built Dugong Hall (the Hall of Great Power) of the Imperial Palace in Shenyang.
1643	16th year, Chongzhen, Sizong	Zhaoling Tomb (Tomb of Huangtaiji, Emperor Taizong of the Qing) was first built in Shenyang, Liaoning.

The Qing Dynasty

1645~1911		The traditional styles of local dwelling houses what we may catch sight of today had been formed to a great extent.
17th century	Early Qing Period	Tomb of Apak Hoja (Khwaja) in Kashi, Xinjiang, was first built. The tomb underwent several renovations in later years.
1644~1661	Reign Period of Shunzhi, Shizu	The West Imperial Garden (the Three Imperial Lakes with their surroundings) was reconstructed west of the Forbidden City in Beijing. The White Dagoba was erected on the top of the hill of the Jade Flower Islet in the Northern Lake (present-day Beihai Park).
1645	2nd year, Shunzhi, Shizu	Dalai Lama the Fifth rebuilt and extended the Potala Palace in Lhasa, Tibet.
1655	12th year, Shunzhi, Shizu	The Palace of Heavenly Purity and Palace of Earthly Tranquillity of the Forbidden City in Beijing were rebuilt.
1661	18th year, Shunzhi, Shizu	The Eastern Qing Tomb in Zunhua, Hebei, began to be constructed.
1662~1722	Reign Period of Kangxi, Shengzu	Chengqi Lou, a circular dwelling of the Hakkas was built in Yongding County, Fujian.
1663	2nd year, Kangxi, Shengzu	Xiaoling Tomb (the Mausoleum of Emperor Shunzhi) was completed in the Eastern Qing Tombs in Zunhua, Hebei.
1672	11th year, Kangxi, Shengzu	Temple of Marquis Wu Xiang in memory of Zhuge Liang was built in Chengdu, Sichuan.
1677	16th year, Kangxi, Shengzu	The layout of Dai Miao (the Temple of Eastern Sacred Mountain) in Mount Tai, Shandong, was completed in today's scale.
1680	19th year, Kangxi, Shengzu	Chengxin Yuan, an imperial garden at Jade Spring Hill in the western suburbs of Beijing, was built. It was renamed as Jingming Yuan, or the Garden of Light and Tranquillity, in later years.
1681	20th year, Kangxi, Shengzu	Jingling Tomb (the Mausoleum of Emperor Kangxi) started to be constructed in the Eastern Qing Tombs in Zunhua, Hebei.
1683	22nd year, Kangxi, Shengzu	Building complex of the Hall of Literary Glory in the Forbidden City in Beijing was rebuilt.
1684	23rd year, Kangxi, Shengzu	Changchun Yuan, or the Enjoying-the-Spring Garden, was constructed in the western suburbs of Beijing.
1689	28th year, Kangxi, Shengzu	Palace of Tranquil Longevity in the Forbidden City in Beijing was built.
1690	29th year, Kangxi, Shengzu	The Hall of Supreme Harmony in the Forbidden City began to be rebuilt. The Hall was completed in 1695.
1703	42nd year, Kangxi, Shengzu	Construction of the Summer Resort at Chengde, Hebei, started.
1710	49th year, Kangxi, Shengzu	Guan Di Miao, or the Temple of Lord Guan was rebuilt in Guan's birthplace Xiexian County, Shanxi.
1718	57th year, Kangxi, Shengzu	Xiaodongling Tomb (the Tomb of Empress of Shunzhi) was built to the east of Xiaoling Tomb in the Eastern Qing Tombs in Zunhua, Hebei.
1725	3rd year, Yongzheng, Shizong	Construction of Yuanming Yuan, or the Garden of Perfect Splendor, or Garden of Perfection and Brightness, started in the northwestern suburbs of Beijing. It was then extended and developed to 40 scenic spots during the period of Emperor Qianlong.
1730	8th year, Yongzheng, Shizong	Tailing Tomb (the Mausoleum of Emperor Yongzheng) was first built-day in Yizhou (present-day Yixian, Hebei). The Tomb was completed in 1737.
1734	12th year, Yongzheng, Shizong	The Board of Works promulgated Gongcheng Zuofa Zeli, or the Structural Regulations, as building codes for design and construction works.
1735	13th year, Yongzheng, Shizong	Fragrant Hill Summer Resort for the emperor was built in the Western Hills of Beijing.
1736~1796	Reign period of Qianlong, Gaozong	Ge Yuliang, a well-known rockery craftsman, built the Huanxiu Shanzhuang (the Nestling-in-Green Mountain Villa) in Suzhou.

Christian era	Chinese Dynastic Years	Events or Achievements
1 7 4 5	1 0th year, Qianlong, Gaozong	Fragrant Hill Summer Resort in the western hills of Beijing was extended and renamed as Jingyi Yuan (the Garden of Congenial Tranquillity).
1746~1748	11th~13th years, Qianlong, Gaozong	The Central Palatial Complex of the Imperial Palace in Shenyang was extended. Two lodges, or building compounds, were built and added to the east and west of the Central Complex.
1750	15th year, Qianlong, Gaozong	The Pavilion of the Rain of Flowers was erected in the Forbidden City in Beijing. Construction of Qingyi Yuan, or the Garden of Clear Ripples, started. It was an imperial garden including the Hill of Longevity and the Kunming Lake in the western suburbs of Beijing. It took 14 years to complete this garden.
1751	16th year, Qianlong, Gaozong	Changchun Yuan (the Garden of Eternal Spring) and Qichun Yuan (the Garden of Blossoming Spring) were built to the east of Yuanming Yuan (the Garden of Perfect Splendor).
1752	17th year, Qianlong, Gaozong	Roofing tiles of the Hall of Prayer for Good Harvest in the Temple of Heaven, Beijing, were rebuilt with blue glazed tiles. The Imperial Palace in Shenyang was renovated.
1755	20th year, Qianlong, Gaozong	Puning Si (Temple of Universal Tranquillity), in Chengde, Hebei, was built. Its main hall, Dacheng Ge (Pavilion of Mahayana) was built to imitate the main hall of Sangye Temple in Tibet.
1764	29th year, Qianlong, Gaozong	Anyuan Miao Temple in Chengde, Hebei, was Built.
1765	30th year, Qianlong, Gaozong	Song Zongyuan, a retired official, built Wangshi Yuan, or the Garden of the Master of Fishing Nets, in Suzhou.
1766	31st year, Qianlong,	Pule Si Temple in Chengde, Hebei, was built.
1767~1771	32nd~36th years, Qianlong, Gaozong	Temple of the Potaraka Doctrine (Pumo Zongcheng Zhi Miao) in Chengde, Hebei, was built.
1774	39th year, Qianlong, Gaozong	Wenyuan Ge Library in the Forbidden City, Beijing, was built.
1778	43rd year, Qianlong, Gaozong	The Western Palatial Complex of the Imperial Palace in Shenyang was built. The Mosque with Su Gong Tower in Turpan, Xinjiang, was completed.
1779~1780	44th~45th years, Qianlong, Gaozong	Temple of Sumeru Happiness and Longevity (Xu Mi Fu Shou Zhi Miao) in Chengde, Hebei, was built.
1781	46th year, Qianlong, Gaozong	Wensu Ge Library, Yangxi Zhai Study and Jiayin Tang Hall of the Imperial Palace in Shenyang were built.
1783	48th year, Qianlong, Gaozong	Biyong, or the Main Hall of the Imperial College (Guo Zi Jian), in Beijing was built.
1784	49th year, Qianlong, Gaozong	Dagobas of the City of Complete Purification (Qing Jing Hua Cheng Ta) of the West Yellow Temple in Beijing were erected.
18th century		Taer Temple in Huangzhong, Qinghai, was built.
1796	1st year, Jiaqing, Renzong	Changling Tomb (the Mausoleum of Emperor Jiaqing) of t h e We s t e r n Qi n g Tombs in Yixian, Hebei, was first built. It was completed eight years later.
1804	9th year, Jiaqing, Renzong	Three Palatial Complexes with Lodges of the Central Complex of the Imperial Palace in Shenyang were renovated.
1832	12th year, Daoguang, Renzong	Muling Tomb (the Mausoleum of Emperor Daoguang) of the Western Qing Tombs in Yixian, Hebei, was first built. It was completed four years later.
1859	9th year, Xianfeng, Wenzong	Dingling Tomb (the Mausoleum of Emperor Xianfeng) of the Eastern Qing Tombs in Zunhua, Hebei, was first built.
1860	10th year, Xianfeng, Wenzong	Yuanming Yuan (the Garden of Perfect Splendor) and Qingyi Yuan (the Garden of Clear Ripples) were destroyed and burnt down by the Anglo-French Allied forces.
1873	12th year, Tongzhi, Muzong	Dingdongling Tombs (Tombs of Empress Dowagers Cixi and Ci'an) were first built in the Eastern Qing Tombs in Zunhua, Hebei. The Tombs were completed in 1879.
1875	1st year, Guangxu, Dezong	Huiling Tomb (the Mausoleum of Emperor Tongzhi) of the Eastern Qing Tombs in Zunhua, Hebei, was built.
1888	14th year, Guangxu, Dezong	Qingyi Yuan was rebuilt and renamed as Yihe Yuan (the Summer Palace) u n d e r Empress Dowager Cixi. Jianfu Palace of Qingcheng Mountain, Sichuan, was rebuilt.
1909	1st year, Xuantong	Chongling Tomb (the Mausoleum of Emperor Guangxu) was built in the Western Qing Tombs in Yixian, Hebei.

The Excellence of Ancient Chinese Architecture, Chinese Edition
Author: Cheng Liyao
Chief Planner: Zhou Yi
Editorial Members: Wang Boyang, Wei Ran, Wang Xuelin
Editor in Charge:Wang Boyang, Zhang Zhenguang, Fei Hailing
Photographers: Zhang Zhenguang, Wei Ran, Chen Xiaoli, Li Dongxi, Cao Yang

The Excellence of Ancient Chinese Architecture, English Edition
Chief Planner: Zhang Huizhen
Translators: Zhang Long, San Mu
Editor in Charge: Qi Linlin, Zhang Huizhen
Photographers: Zhang Zhenguang, Wei Ran, Chen Xiaoli, Li Dongxi, Cao Yang
Cover Design: Fu Jinhong
Layout Design: Xiao Jinxing

The Excellence of
Ancient Chinese Architecture

Private Gardens 介尺園林建築
Gardens for the Enjoyment of Artificial Landscapes of Men of Letters

Cheng Liyao

© 2012 China Architecture & Building Press
Published and Distributed by China Architecture & Building Press
ISBN 978-7-112-13972-9 (22005)
CIP data available on request
www.cabp.com.cn

Printed on acid-free and chlorine-free bleached paper

Printed in China